T0152335

THE
FEMINIST
FINANCIAL
$ HANDBOOK $

Copyright © 2018 Brynne Conroy

Published by Mango Publishing Group, a division of Mango Media Inc.

Cover and Layout Design: Elina Diaz

Mango is an active supporter of authors' rights to free speech and artistic expression in their books. The purpose of copyright is to encourage authors to produce exceptional works that enrich our culture and our open society.

Uploading or distributing photos, scans or any content from this book without prior permission is theft of the author's intellectual property. Please honor the author's work as you would your own. Thank you in advance for respecting our author's rights.

For permission requests, please contact the publisher at:

Mango Publishing Group
2850 Douglas Road, 3rd Floor
Coral Gables, FL 33134 U.S.A.
info@mango.bz

For special orders, quantity sales, course adoptions and corporate sales, please email the publisher at sales@mango.bz. For trade and wholesale sales, please contact Ingram Publisher Services at: customer.service@ingramcontent.com or +1.800.509.4887.

The Feminist Financial Handbook: A Modern Woman's Guide to a Wealthy Life

Library of Congress Cataloging

ISBN: (print) 978-1-63353-808-5 (ebook) 978-1-63353-809-2
Library of Congress Control Number: 2018952303
BISAC category code: BUS050000—BUSINESS & ECONOMICS / Personal Finance / General

Printed in the United States of America

THE
FEMINIST
FINANCIAL
$ HANDBOOK $

A Modern Woman's Guide to a Wealthy Life

Brynne Conroy

mango

CORAL GABLES

Praise for *The Feminist Financial Handbook*

"Conroy is an awesome writer and fierce feminist."

—**Emily Guy Birken**, author of *End Financial Stress Now*

"*The Feminist Financial Handbook* is a unicorn among finance books—one that endeavors to recontextualize sensible financial basics within an acknowledgment of the myriad forms of oppression within our society. I wholeheartedly applaud Brynne Conroy in her efforts to transform both the role of the finance information world as it exists and the inequalities of the world. Brava!"

—**Becca Anderson**, author of *The Book of Awesome Women* and *Badass Affirmations*

"In *The Feminist Financial Handbook*, Brynne Conroy provides women with a comprehensive guide to living a wealthier life that contains actionable advice while not sugarcoating real issues that impact women such as the gender pay gap and the impact of divorce. This book is a valuable read."

—**David Carlson**, author of *Hustle Away Debt* and founder of Young Adult Money

"One of the leading voices in personal finance, Brynne Conroy perfectly sums up what it means to be a woman in the twenty-first century. Money affects every part of our lives—from the way we dress to how we can support ourselves and our families—and Conroy does a perfect job of highlighting how the pay gap, discrimination, and the motherhood penalty affect women's money differently. This is the perfect book for the modern woman looking to understand her finances on a societal level (and how to fight back)."

—**Tori Dunlap**, editor at Tomorrow Ideas

"Too often, we forget that women have very unique financial needs. *The Feminist Financial Handbook* remedies this problem nicely by tackling issues modern women face when planning for a secure financial future. If you're a woman struggling with the reality of money in the patriarchy, this book can help you break free and live your best financial life."

—**Miranda Marquit**, money expert, financial journalist, and political activist

"Conroy has done her research and given a platform to the rich and diverse experiences of womanhood and our relationship to money. This truly is the feminist financial handbook for the new wave of intersectional feminism."

—**Erin Lowry**, author of *Broke Millennial: Stop Scraping By and Get Your Financial Life Together*

"Conroy goes beyond blanket, modern-day notions of #girlboss to not only explore, but redefine what financial well-being means to different people. Meticulously researched, forward-thinking, and contemporarily feminist—which includes ableism and non-traditional populations—*The Feminist Financial Handbook* not only serves as a practical guide, but as a platform of empowerment to the oppressed and underserved."

—**Jackie Lam**, owner of Hello Freelancer

To my children.

TABLE OF CONTENTS

FOREWORD

In the kitchen of my childhood home, my mother kept a poster of the famous "We Can Do It!" Rosie the Riveter image in a prominent spot. My sister and I grew up eating our Cheerios and Pop Tarts under the benevolent gaze of Rosie, eternally rolling up her sleeves to get shit done.

It was no accident that Rosie enjoyed such pride of place in Mom's house. My mother wanted to make sure my sister and I both understood that we could do anything we put our minds to. She hoped we would learn early on that women are strong and capable, despite social messages that would make us feel less-than, just because we were girls. Our Rosie poster was part of Mom's pushback against a patriarchal system that so often keeps women from achieving their full potential.

But even though the examples and lessons I learned at my mother's knee (and Rosie's portrait) were important, formative, and feminist, they did not go far enough.

For instance, though I learned as a child that women earned eighty cents for every man's dollar, I did not understand that the larger gap facing women of color must be highlighted rather than treated as a footnote.

Though I knew I would likely face discrimination as a woman, I did not understand the intersectional ways in which I was privileged as a straight, white, abled, cisgender woman.

And though I believed in the importance of financial equality for women, I did not understand the ways that I benefited from other types of financial inequality.

In short, I did not understand that financial choices grew more constricted the less you looked like the iconic, glamorous, white woman we call Rosie the Riveter. Rosie is supposed to represent women's strength, but an image that pigeonholes women into a specific physical appearance is no way to celebrate and inspire all women.

I start with all of this to explain why I was so delighted to see an updated version of Rosie gracing the cover of my friend Brynne Conroy's new book, *The Feminist Financial Handbook*—which you now hold in your hands.

With this book, Brynne has created something that we desperately need: she has written a handbook on finances from a feminist perspective, and she invites *all* women and non-binary individuals to create a new financial future for themselves within it. Her commitment to intersectionality in this feminist handbook is represented by the Rosie of color on the cover, inviting all women, not just white women, to identify with this iconic image of feminine strength.

You can always find books geared toward helping women to improve their financial lives. Some are condescending, mansplanations of finance, couched as an important help to us little ladies and our emotional lady-brains. Some offer pink-jacketed rah-rah enthusiasm claiming to help the modern woman "*have it all!*" Some are deep dives into the real financial difficulties and challenges facing specific groups of women. But none of them look at finance from an intersectional feminist perspective—until now.

As you read through *The Feminist Financial Handbook*, Brynne will walk you through the unique financial challenges and concerns facing women in the US and Canada. Many of these issues will be ones you are familiar with (and pretty damn sick of), and Brynne's explanations and recommendations will give you new tools for dealing with old problems.

Other issues will be surprising to you, often because they either do not affect you personally, or because you have never had the specific language to describe or discuss them. You will also learn excellent options for mitigating those issues that were once invisible or surprising and are still largely unrecognized by our society as a whole.

To illustrate many of the challenges facing women in our society, Brynne also includes stories and interviews with several women who have created fulfilling and meaningful lives for themselves despite facing major financial, social, health-related, and sexist obstacles. These women have found ways to hold onto their money, dignity, hope, and joy in some truly difficult situations, and their examples can help others who face similar rocky paths.

In every chapter, Brynne offers both actionable steps and hope for individual women who want to improve both their lives and their finances. She offers suggestions for how to fight the unfair system while also working within the system. That means everyone who reads this book will put it down knowing ways to work for both a better world as a whole and a better life as an individual.

We all need to fight for a world in which financial equality is the norm—and we all need to individually work to improve our own financial lives. That may sound like a tall order, but as the Rosie of my childhood proclaimed, "We can do it!" Motivated women working together can accomplish damn near anything.

So let's roll up our sleeves and get some serious shit done.

Emily Guy Birken

Nasty woman and bestselling author of *End Financial Stress Now, Making Social Security Work for You,* and *The 5 Years Before You Retire*

INTRODUCTION

"What's so different about women's money?"

It's a question I get asked frequently. And the answer is almost everything. While it's true that numbers and math don't care about your gender, numbers and math are hardly the driving force behind personal finances. Instead, outside cultural influences often affect our financial situations more than we'd like to admit.

Let's take salary, for example. Both in the United States and Canada, there is a substantial gender pay gap. When women are doing the same jobs as men, they're making less money for it—except in a few select fields which remain unionized. If we take a step back from salary and look at just landing a job in the first place, everything from your gender presentation to your race to your accent can affect whether you get your foot in the door during an interview or not.

Even when we look at aspects of personal finance that we would think are more within the realm of our own control, internalized prejudice can taint our behavior. We may blow off a shopping spree as nothing because that's just how women cope with stress according to society. This is despite the fact that men and women are nearly equally likely to be shopaholics. One of the women I interviewed for this book noted that she frequently heard people in her community brushing off their bad credit scores because, "All black people have bad credit."

Whether we're looking at internal or external oppression, those who would preach that numbers and math are all there is between you and a magical, early retirement at some ungodly age are wrong. They are likely oozing with privilege that blinds them to difficult realities which they themselves have never had to face. Or if they've worked their way out from a childhood of poverty themselves, they make an assumption that anyone else can do it, too, despite the fact that we all live under diverse and complex circumstances—even when we live in poverty.

That's why this book exists. It takes a deeper look at economic inequality as it applies to earning, managing, and saving money within the context of oppression. It features the stories and advice of women who have looked the reality of these related struggles square in the face as well as the coping mechanisms they have used to either conquer or push through these challenges. You'll find that their anecdotes are at the heart of this work; I am eternally grateful for their openness, their willingness, and the time they dedicated to this project. Please check out their information in the back of this book to find out where you can see more of their work. I mean, actually do it. Their voices are important and eye-opening. You won't regret it.

Because I don't want to utterly depress you, we're also going to talk about ways you can work within existing systems. Prejudice and oppression are both horrendous, but unfortunately, they're not going away any time soon. We have some long battles ahead of us. So we'll look at some work-arounds that may help you propel your personal finances to that next level within the oppressive systems in which we live.

Before we dive in, there are a few terms I want to review. Feminism is widely recognized, and in recent years intersectional feminism has started to see some of the spotlight. But because these things are not discussed in all circles, I know there's some vocabulary in these pages that might look foreign to some readers.

Intersectional Feminism: If feminism focuses on the oppression and equality of women, intersectional feminism focuses on the same for all oppressed groups. For example, you could be a white male who grew up in poverty. You'd be privileged because you're male and white, but oppressed because of the economic situation you grew up in. You could be a black disabled woman from a wealthy family, inheriting the privilege that comes along with wealth, but facing deep oppression because of your race, gender, and the incapability others project onto you. We all have parts of our life that intersect with both privilege and oppression; the ratio is different for each one of us, though.

Kyriarchy: You know how the patriarchy is essentially an institutionalized and culturally accepted act of men ruling over women? Think of the kyriarchy in the same way, except instead of just men ruling over women, it's also Europeans colonizing native lands while committing genocide and raping native women, white people exercising systemic racism even a century and half after they ended slavery without paying reparations, disabled people being thought of as incapable, and transgender people facing employment discrimination and sometimes even fear of death simply for living an authentic life; and the list goes on. Any type of institution and/or oppression that exists, that says one group is better than the other and therefore deserves more rights, privileges, and protections, is a part of the kyriarchy.

Heteronormativity: Heteronormativity is the dangerous assumption that everyone is heterosexual. While homophobia is an active fear of those who are attracted to the same sex, heteronormativity is a quieter and sometimes more insidious form of prejudice based on one's sexual orientation. For example, someone with heteronormative values may not see how equal marriage is a moral issue outside of their own religious beliefs. They might repeatedly call your partner, wife, or husband your "friend" despite knowing full well the context of your relationship. It's a series of aggressions that oppress those who are anything other than heterosexual.

Cisnormativity: Being cisgender means you identify with the gender you were assigned at birth. So cisnormativity is the dangerous assumption that everyone is cisgender. When you have cisnormative values, you might not want to allow people the dignity of going to the bathroom of the gender with which they identify. You may not want transgender people to serve in the military because their identity makes you uncomfortable and you want to punish them for it. It's a damaging failure to recognize those who are not cisgender as full human beings.

Disablism: Abled people like to feel bad for disabled people and turn them into pet projects. But they like to complain when disabled people get pushed to the front of the line or when laws force them to spend a little money to make their business establishments accessible. They like to threaten sweeping cuts to Medicaid and Medicare—systems that help disabled people to live full lives and sometimes even to stay alive at all—because why should they have to pay for someone else's health care? When abled people are doing these things, they are practicing disablism. They fail to see that just because someone can't complete the same tasks in the same ways as themselves, it doesn't mean they don't have different and meaningful ways to contribute to society.

This book focuses on women's money, the ways in which the kyriarchy oppresses and affects that money, and economic coping mechanisms that might help make things better for you until that kyriarchy falls. We'll talk about wealth, the different ways in which we define it, and how you can live a life full of contentment regardless of your current money situation.

As you read these women's stories, I hope you learn as much as I did. They have found some awe-inspiring ways to build meaningful lives while striving towards economic freedom.

PART ONE

DEFINING WEALTH

CHAPTER 1

I Can Have It All—Can't I?

In short, no, you can't.

As women, we often pursue "having it all." We're supposed to have careers, be fantastic moms who raise our children with grace, and participate in community volunteer efforts. Oh, and we're supposed to look great while we're doing all this.

If you look at the women in your life who supposedly have it all, I'm willing to bet they have stuff going on behind the scenes that you don't see: a nanny; a personal assistant; a family member who is there supporting them. And I guarantee there's still stress. They may just not show it publicly.

Yet we look at the Instagram feeds of these "superwomen" and judge ourselves against them. We get down on ourselves because we're not succeeding in every last arena. Maybe you're struggling to balance work and family. Maybe you haven't met the right person with whom to settle down and start a family—or maybe a family isn't something you want at all. Perhaps despite your best efforts, you've struggled to get your career off the ground. Or maybe in the craziness of everyday life, you've let yourself go, and society won't let you forget about it.

We all have areas in our lives where we feel deficient. Not one of us is perfect at everything, and some of us have more resources at our disposal to ameliorate those areas of imperfection, while others do not. Not one of us ever truly grasps onto the illusive "balance" we're seeking—the balance we're told by countless self-help books and gurus that we can achieve.

I'm here to tell you that's okay. In fact, as suggested by Stanford Economics professor Myra Strober,[1] we're probably better off dropping the concept of "balance" altogether. It's almost never achievable, and we make ourselves miserable in its pursuit.

THE CONCEPT OF SHIFTING PRIORITIES

I was brought up in a religious household. The religion was strict and all-consuming. I kid you not when I tell you that as a teen, I spent ten hours at church per week over the course of six days. And that was if there wasn't a baptism or youth project or some other type of celebratory event.

I no longer practice the religion of my youth, but there were good things I received in that environment. While some people were absolutely crazy and judgmental, there were plenty of churchgoers I liked and respected. Some of the deepest life lessons I have learned were taught to me by these mentors.

For example, one Sunday, we were sitting in the third hour of church—the hour designated for the teenage-girls-only lesson. One of my favorite teachers was standing in front of the class as we sat with our scriptures under our chairs and our skirt-clad legs pressed firmly together.

She was teaching us about time management and prioritization. I don't know if the lesson was from the manual or was just something she wanted us to learn. Whatever the origins, she wrote these four words on the board:

- *Family*
- *Church*
- *School*
- *Friends*

You can replace the word "school" with "work," if it better fits your situation. And "church" with "giving back" or "volunteering."

She explained to us that at different points in our lives, we'd rank each of these areas differently in terms of importance. Because we were in church that day, she knew that part of the equation was important to us. Because we were teenagers, she ascertained that "friends" were likely one of the focal points of our lives, too. While some of us put a high priority on school, others did not.

She noted that at the stage of life she was in, as a homemaker with young children, family was higher up on her list than ever. Church and friends were important, too, but her kids took precedence, so that's where she spent the most time. At that juncture in her life, she wasn't overly concerned with a specific career outside the home.

She explained that as she got older, these four priorities might shift around again. Then, she said something transformational:

"You know what? *That's okay.*"

In that moment, she gave us permission to not be all things at once. She didn't tell us spirituality or charity should always be our number one priority; she encouraged us to recognize that at different stages of our lives, our priorities would change.

And that there was nothing wrong with that.

AN EXERCISE IN PRIORITIZATION

Now that you know there's nothing wrong with prioritizing rather than being all things at once, sit down with yourself and get real about what's important in your own life. Keep in mind that the way you prioritize shouldn't be based on the way things have been in the past or on the way others live their lives. Your prioritization is going to be personal and based on your current situation, and it should be free from judgement—even your own.

I want you to think about five areas:

- *Family*
- *Friends*
- *Work/School*
- *Volunteer/Community Efforts*
- *Personal Goal*

Your personal goal may be related to a hobby, travel or something else entirely.

Now, you're going to rank these in order of importance to you at this current point in time. Remember that there is no wrong or right order.

1. _____

2. _____

3. _____

4. _____

5. _____

Whatever's on your fifth line, it's not a priority in your life right now. You can still have it, but don't spend too much effort on it at this very moment.

Instead, focus your energies on lines one and two, with gradually decreasing effort on lines three and four.

It's important to note that while there is no wrong or right order for your priorities, you may have to adjust them based on reality. For example, if you don't have a partner who is providing and/or you're not financially independent, you're going to have a hard time if your first two line items are friends and personal goals with "work" listed on line number five. You do need some sort of money or income to facilitate your efforts in other areas, so you may have to move work up higher—even if you don't want to.

GOING WITH THE FLOW

Over a decade later, I was sitting at a roundtable brainstorming session with some strong, inspiring women. We were trying to address the stressors that come along with motherhood, especially for working mothers. Some of us worked full-time while others worked part-time. While there was a mother or two who contended she had actually found the illusive balance, most of us agreed that there was no winning. There was no perfectly clean house owned by a woman doting on her perfectly-behaved small children while running her small business like a well-oiled machine, at least not at all times.

Then, our wise discussion leader brought up the idea of flow. Flow basically means going with what's working well. Yes, maybe your dishes have been piling up for a week, but you've done $5,000 in sales. It's your busy time of year, so you don't sweat the dishes and keep pushing forward with your efforts at work.

Or maybe you've decided you want to stay home with the kids, and you are fortunate enough to be able to pursue this decision. Your career is on pause for the moment, but you're able to organize amazing birthday parties with homemade decorations and a cake baked from scratch.

When we go with the flow, we acknowledge our priorities and are able to complete the tasks in front of us with higher efficiency. When we try to achieve balance, we end up overwhelmed, with the stress making it harder to get anything done with as much competency.

That night, I synthesized the ideas in front of me with that lesson I had learned in church all those years ago. When we know our priorities, we can focus our efforts on the things that matter most to us in that moment. When we focus on flow rather than trying to balance all of our different priorities, we're better able to concentrate and get in the zone as we work on the parts of our life that are highest up on the list at any given moment. We're more likely to do a better job, build confidence in our own abilities, and feel fulfilled in our purpose. All of these things lead to contentment and less stress.

WHAT DOES THIS HAVE TO DO WITH MONEY?

If all this is feeling rather squishy to you, rest assured that there are hard numbers involved. When we choose our careers over becoming a homemaker or even having a family at all, it inherently impacts how much money we're bringing in every month. Making this decision increases our cashflow and allows us to avoid those dreaded resume gaps that so many claim are to blame for the gender pay gap.

But choosing to be a homemaker is just as valid of a decision. Maybe you ran the numbers and you'd essentially be working to put your kids in daycare. Maybe you'd make enough, but you've decided you'd feel more fulfilled raising children and keeping house 24/7. Or maybe you and your spouse have decided it will go the other way around: your spouse will stay home while you work.

Foregoing childbearing—whether in favor of a career or not—is just as valid a decision as having kids. You give up a lot of freedom when you become a parent, and knowing that's not something you want to sacrifice is a mature and rational decision.

Remember that feminism is about equal access to choices. Your priorities are just that: yours. They're not anyone else's, and if others judge you for them, that's their problem—not yours. You can be a feminist homemaker or a CEO, or you can spend your time wandering the world as a digital nomad. All of these are valid choices. The goals of feminism are to make all these options available to you and to have the decision to pursue any particular route be made by you and your partner if you have one—not by outside cultural pressures.

You cannot be all things to all people at once. As empowering of a concept as it's meant to be, in reality, there is no superwoman. We're all just imperfect beings trying to make the best decisions possible relative to the context of our own lived experience.

We can better do that when we recognize we will never be omnipotent. When we prioritize and release some of the stress of being all things at all times, we are actually doing a lot to help our bottom line. A 2014 study at the University of Michigan revealed that women going through acute stress saw an income decrease of 18 percent to 30 percent.[2] While we'll never be able to dodge all stress, we can relieve some of it by letting go of the idea of becoming that woman with a perfectly balanced life, and potentially improve our finances while we're at it.

Instead, we can go with the flow, allowing ourselves to live our best lives rather than what we think is the life of the "perfect" woman. Because she doesn't exist.

THE IMPERFECT WEALTHY WOMAN

We've established and accepted that the "perfect" or "super" woman is a myth. But we can still find wealth even with all our perfectly normal imperfections.

Defining wealth is tricky business, though. Traditionally, the word is associated with mountains of money. While that's certainly one aspect of wealth, you can have tons of cash and still be totally miserable. We also need to pay attention to factors like our physical health, mental health, social networks, and overall contentment.

If you're working 60 hours per week in front of a screen, you may have a ton of money but not a ton of physical activity in your life.

You may also be having a hard time connecting with your friends and family because of the scarcity of free time. This is a problem because our social connections play a large role in our mental health and have even been identified as a corollary factor in living a longer life.[3]

And then there is contentment or happiness. This is such a complex topic that the entire next chapter will be dedicated to it. Before we delve into how to be happy, though, take a minute and think about your own values. In much the same way as you prioritize your time, consider how you prioritize these factors as contributing to your overall wealth status. Because a wealthy life isn't all about dollars and cents.

TAKE ACTION ⑤

- *Let go of the idea of superwoman.*

- *Prioritize these five areas of your life:*

  - *Family*

  - *Friends*

  - *Work/School*

  - *Volunteer/Community Efforts*

  - *Personal Goal*

Be sure to rank them in order of importance to you now, not by how important each has been to you in the past. Also make sure you are making these decisions without outside influence.

1. _____

2. _____

3. _____

4. _____

5. _____

- *Before you get into evaluating your money, think about how you are doing in other areas of your life, as these can affect your perception of being your wealthiest self, too. Some examples include physical health, mental health, social networks, and overall contentment.*

CHAPTER II

Money Isn't the Key to Happiness

Stop chasing cash. And stop chasing smiles while you're at it.

We've established that you won't find happiness in having it all—primarily because that's an unachievable goal. We've also identified that happiness or contentment is a primary concern when we're defining what a wealthy life looks like for us as individuals. Despite that, you may be surprised to find out that the reverse isn't necessarily true: the amount of money in your bank account does not dictate your happiness levels.

According to research by positive psychology professor Sonja Lyubomirsky, only about 10 percent of one's happiness level can be attributed to our circumstances.[4] Our circumstances include things like where we live, how we look, and—yes—how much money we make. That means that our income has far less than 10 percent bearing on how content we are in our life.

That being said, not having enough money can lead to higher stress levels. Higher stress obviously makes us less content—or satiated, as scientists phrase it. If you are making $32,000 per year, your satiation levels are highly likely to improve if your household income jumps up to $70,000 per year, since those extra tens of thousands give you the resources you need to make it through daily life and tackle obstacles and emergencies that may come your way with far more ease.

There is a tipping point, though. In 2018, a new study came out with new numbers as to how much is needed to achieve peak money-to-satiation ratios in different areas across the world. Here in North America, that number is $105,000. If your household income is below this amount, more money would likely make you more satiated. Beyond that amount, however, more financial wealth is not worth pursuing if you're trying to use money to bring you contentment.[5]

The most recent government-verified data shows US households have a median income of $59,039 USD per year, while the median Canadian household income is $80,940 CAD per year.[6] This indicates that more than 50 percent of our respective populations would see greater satiation levels if they brought in more money annually.

But remember, income is only one of several factors that contribute to only 10 percent of those satiation levels. More money is going to help, but it's not necessarily going to make your life abundantly joyous.

Where are our efforts better spent? I talked to Carol Graham—Leo Pasvolsky Fellow at The Brookings Institute—to find out. While Graham doesn't tell people how to become happy, she has extensively studied contributing factors to well-being, especially across global populations of women.

MEANINGFUL EXPERIENCES

The American Dream, enshrined in the Declaration of Independence as, 'Life, Liberty, and the Pursuit of Happiness,' may just be toxic in the way we currently interpret it. Because this is a feminist book, we'll take a look at the fact that these words were lifted and altered—and the underlying reasons why.

Thomas Jefferson did indeed steal this phrase from John Locke, an English philosopher who focused on society and politics. The original phrase was 'life, liberty, and property,' but seeing as how Jefferson and several other of the founding fathers counted human slaves as their own property, they couldn't very well get behind the idea that the government was responsible for making sure everyone owned something. After all, in their world orientation, some people were themselves property.

The founding fathers also did not believe that non-landowners should have a voice in democracy. The common reasoning was that those who didn't have property were not as well educated and would vote without having full access to information. In a day when newspapers took forever to circulate and literacy rates were low, the argument nicely ices over the thinly veiled heteronormative, white male fragility which can be found right under the surface of its logic. These men wanted no threat to their power, and they viewed themselves as superior over others despite laying out some the most liberating principles the Western World had seen in quite some time.

The founding fathers eventually gave every white man the ability to vote but hedged their bets by establishing the electoral college—a group of representatives who vote on behalf of your state. To this day, the electoral college can vote either in line with or against what the people of their state *actually* want.

Locke did use the term *"pursuit of happiness"* on a separate occasion, but he viewed it from a very different perspective than we do today. Our capitalistic and individualistic society tends to pursue happiness through material means. That means we pursue money. We pursue the house with the white picket fence, nice cars, and anything we can show off on social media.

Locke, however, saw the pursuit of happiness as using one's own life to contribute to the betterment of society. You needed to be a moral person, steeped in virtue, and willing to forego your own desires in favor of the greater good. It is highly likely that Jefferson had the same interpretation of this phrase, whatever we read into it today.[7]

Although they could not scientifically prove their correctness, Locke and Jefferson were onto something. Today we have data, and Graham says that it clearly shows that those living in a democracy are only more satiated than those who are not if they're active participants in their democracy. Being civically responsible does indeed improve our overall sense of well-being.

"Going out and peacefully marching is a good thing for your well-being," Graham says, offering examples. "Women running for office because they're mad about what's going on is good for women's well-being."

There is real value in getting involved in politics right now rather than throwing your hands up in the air in frustration. Not only can it potentially improve the national plight, but you will receive personal benefits by being more content in your own life.

Politics isn't the only arena where meaningful action can improve your sense of well-being, though. Research shows that simply taking part in meaningful experiences improves your well-being. If you find your work meaningful, you will be more content—particularly if you view it through the lens of benefitting others.[8] If you decide you want to stay at home and throw all of your efforts at family life to the exclusion of remaining in the workforce, you will be more content if there is a deep meaning behind that decision for you. You may find meaning in volunteer work or in any number of other activities.

"Purposeful—or meaningful—experiences are the most important determinant in levels of well-being," explains Graham. "You could be volunteering, staying at home with your kids, or doing research that drives you. You don't do these things to seek happiness. You do them to find fulfilment."

In fact, Graham says that if you are seeking happiness, you're unlikely to find it. All of us naturally fall on a bell curve of innate happiness levels. At the far left are people who tend to be the least satisfied. In the middle are those with average satiation levels in their life. This middle group is the largest. Then, on the far right side of the bell curve are those who tend to be innately optimistic, which may lead to improved work opportunities, social connections, and a better outlook on the future. These are the people who we'd classify as classically happy in our day-to-day vernacular.

"People who try to be happy are usually the least happy people," explains Graham. "If you don't have enough in your own life to drive what you're doing and you're looking for happiness from cheesy magazines, you're by definition in the lower part of the well-being distribution."

That means that you're on the far left side of that bell curve. Graham notes that if you fall on this side of the curve, you're more likely to be focused on things like money or your looks as you think it will improve your circumstances and thus improve your satisfaction with life. But the people on the far right side of that bell curve, who have a natural inclination towards a better sense of well-being, focus their efforts on creativity and learning rather than cash. They innately know that fulfillment and purpose are the keys to finding contentment in this life—regardless of financial circumstances.

It's not easy to be on the far left side of that bell curve, especially in a society that interprets "the pursuit of happiness" as the extremely individualistic pursuit of a higher economic station. But if we look at Locke's original intent with this phrase, we start to see that meaning—whether it's in the civic arena or within our own selves—is what we should truly be pursuing rather than material "happiness."

THE RIGHT PARTNER

Want to move from the left to the right side of that bell curve? For a long time, there's been a myth circulating that marriage makes people happier. It's not void of all truth; data has shown that those who are married tend to be happier.

But correlation does not equate to causation. Graham notes that since this initial myth emerged from studies that looked at one data point at a fixed point in time, new research has revealed that the more innate happiness you have, the more likely you are to get married in the first place. It's not marriage that's making people have a higher sense of well-being; it's a strong sense of well-being that tends to lead to marriage.

"Over time, the effects of getting married fade," says Graham. "The initial euphoria lasts about eighteen months—then they revert to premarriage happiness levels. They're not happier because they're married. They were just happier before they got married."

That does not mean that if you're on the left side of the bell curve you can't find love. A 2009 study called *'You Can't Be Happier Than Your Wife'*[9] revealed that a gap in happiness levels is a major predictor for divorce. All that means is that when one partner has noticeably higher happiness levels when compared to the other, the marriage isn't likely to last.

The kicker here is that the wife must be the one further to the right side of the bell curve. If she's less happy than her husband or long-term male partner, the marriage is less likely to last. If the male partner is less happy, the same effect isn't there.

So go find a partner who shares a similar level of happiness with you if you want a long marriage. Because you're a woman, though, you're more likely to be okay if you find a man who is to the left of you on the well-being bell curve.

Apologies for the heteronormative study. Hopefully since marriage has been legalized for all, we'll start seeing similar studies for the LGBTQIA+ community.

GENDER'S SURPRISING ROLE IN WELL-BEING

Your perception of your own well-being is affected differently by outside circumstances when you're a woman. I'm excited to let you know this is one of the pieces of good news you'll find in this oppression-focused book!

Major shocks to gender roles in a culture can mess with our well-being. For example, Graham notes that the women's liberation movement—the time period when women were finally able to enter the workforce—sparked a decrease in women's happiness levels. The initial shift in gender expectations was rocky, but she also says that in America, our happiness levels have greatly recovered since this time period.

"Women are happier than men unless they're in a place where gender rights are severely hampered," says Graham. She harkens back to being an active participant in your democracy, noting that movements such as #MeToo or #SheShouldRun have actually been good for women's well-being. They're a sign that more rights are being shifted to women, and that they're empowered enough to take meaningful action. Fifty years ago, women were socially shunned when they empowered themselves by taking on work. Today, they're applauded for their bravery when they tell their stories of how those workplaces have been abusive. When women run for office because they want to change the current system, many of them are getting voted in.

Women are also able to handle personal shocks better than men. Graham hypothesizes that because we're expected to wear so many hats, something like job loss doesn't affect us as negatively; we're able to carry on because our identities are so multifaceted. Men, on the other hand, have traditionally been valued based on their ability to provide. Thus, when they lose their jobs, their entire identities tend to be threatened or even shattered.

This may change as equality becomes more widespread and gender norms continue to become more progressive. But for the time being, women who must go through economic shocks fare much better in terms of overall happiness than their male counterparts.

THE RIGHT ATTITUDE

When we talk about Graham's bell curve, it's important to note that the graph measures people's innate happiness regardless of their circumstances. Education, marriage, income levels, and other circumstances do not play a role in whether you fall closer to the left side or the right.

"People in the happiest part [the right side] are there regardless of income level," explains Graham. "The least happy people are there [the left side] regardless of income. We know this income coefficient matters a lot more to those who are the least happy."

That means that the less happy you are, the more likely you are to focus on money rather than creativity or learning. For most households today, income levels are variable, riding ups and downs rather than going perpetually up in a straight line.[10] That means as your income varies, you'll be more focused on the dollars and cents, how unfair life has been to you during the down times, and all the reasons life hasn't worked out the way you hoped. Conversely, if you're focused on creativity, learning, and purpose, those ups and downs in income levels are less likely to feel so nauseating. You're more likely to have an optimistic outlook on life, and it will be easier to keep going as your life will have meaning beyond how much is in your bank account.

Graham has measured how big of an impact this optimism can have on life outcomes. Perhaps unsurprisingly, those who fall on the right side of the bell curve tend to do better for themselves in an array of different areas. Graham notes that this difference in orientation and attitude can be particularly pronounced for those who do not have a lot of money to start with.

"People with higher levels of this innate happiness do better in the job market," says Graham. "They're healthier. And they do better in the social arena. Innate happiness means more to people with less means. If you think about it, if you're young and just starting out or lower down in the service sector, a good attitude is going to matter a lot to how you do in the labor market versus if you got a PhD in physics—even if you're a curmudgeon, you're probably going to get a good job [with such a PhD].

"In the health care arena, people who are more upbeat deal better with chronic illnesses. I mean, if you have terminal cancer, you have terminal cancer. But there are a lot of diseases and conditions that require some determination to either live with or overcome. Even with harder illnesses, to get through a hard course of treatment, that positive attitude on the margin matters—a lot.

"In the social arena, it's pretty obvious. Do you want to hang out with someone who's cheerful and happy, or do you want to hang out with curmudgeons?"

As someone who worries, works hard to head off potential bad outcomes because of those worries, and writes about money for a living, it may be safe to say I'm one of those curmudgeons—or at least closer to the left side of the curve than the right.

While we do not know for sure if we can change our innate happiness levels, having this information makes me feel more at peace. It helps me know that my tendencies towards resilience are to my advantage, and that if I were able to change my core attitude towards what's coming up ahead—perhaps becoming more of an optimist than the realist I currently am—I might be able to see tangible results in my life.

That's not to say it's a guarantee. But to me, it lets me know that when I actively choose to be more optimistic, I'm upping my odds of success. I may not reach success in the way I had envisioned, and I may hit patches where my nature wins out over my will to be more positive. But perhaps I can at least improve my odds by purposefully correcting my perspective when I notice myself getting too bogged down by the inequity of this experience called life.

TAKE ACTION 💲

- *Stop trying to find happiness. Instead, look for purpose and meaning in your life.*

- *Make a list of things that give you purpose outside of earning an income.*

- *Make a list of the people who your work helps. This could be anyone from your coworkers to your children to society at large.*

- *What is something you'd like to learn more about? Make a conscious goal to learn more about it this week. Do the same the following week until indulging your curiosities has become a habit.*

- *Identify one way you'd like to participate in your democracy. You don't have to run for office, and there are things you can do even on those occasions when there aren't any marches. Find one that has meaning for you, and commit to following through with action.*

CHAPTER III

But Poverty Sure Can Rain on Your Parade

One in three women lives in or on the brink of poverty.

We have now learned that money isn't the key to happiness, but let's not get too blasé about it. Because remember, if you're living below that $105,000 annual income level, more money *is* going to improve your lot in life.

This is an especially important fact for women. According to The Shriver Report, one in three American women live in or on the brink of poverty. In this same report, we learn that two-thirds of minimum wage workers are women who often operate without sick days, and two-thirds of American women are the primary or co-breadwinners for their families.[11] Twenty-five percent of native women live in poverty—more than any other racial group. These same women are increasingly becoming the breadwinners in their families as they attain higher education levels and pursue managerial positions at a higher rate.[12] In Canada, 10 percent of women live in poverty, and 1.5 million women live on a low income.[13]

This systemic problem is complex, and it is likely best addressed at the systemic level. However, if we're going to fix this issue as a society, we have to recognize it exists and recognize the unfounded prejudices towards the poor in an individualistic society.

Nicole Lynn Perry, an activist in Seattle, Washington, has struggled greatly with poverty and has seen these prejudices firsthand. Her financial situation led her and her then-wife to make some risky financial decisions. Perry had just separated from the military and was having trouble finding work back in her hometown of Dallas, Texas, despite her best efforts. The only income she was bringing in was a little bit of money from the Post-9/11 GI Bill.

Without a steady income, banks wouldn't lend the couple the money they needed to get by, so they turned to payday loans, which they took out under Perry's name. They were never able to pay off these predatory loans. This is extremely common and should serve as a warning to all to stay away from these loans if at all humanly possible. The payday loans ultimately ended up being one of the biggest negative line items on her credit report.

It wasn't *just* the payday loans, though. Perry and her ex were so desperate for money to get by that they used even more unconventional methods to get cash for the bills through their credit union.

"If you had a fraudulent charge on your card, you could claim it and they'd temporarily give you the money," Perry explains. "If the claim was legit, you got to keep the money. If they found out your claim was a bad one and you had actually made the purchase, you'd have to pay the money back."

Perry and her wife made somewhere between five and ten claims, knowing that the charges weren't fraudulent. They needed the money to survive. But when the credit union came knocking, wanting their money back for the legitimate charges, Perry didn't have it. She lost her account, and her credit took another hit.

Later, her poor credit history would prevent her from renting an apartment. A poor credit score can make it extremely difficult to get by in many areas. You might not be able to get an auto loan for that vehicle you desperately need in order to drive to work. You're more likely to get turned down for a mortgage, and some employers will even refuse to hire you if your score is too low or your credit history is too spotty.

Perry knows she made mistakes. But she was also doing the best she could at the time with the extremely limited resources she had available to her.

"Just because we're low- or middle-income doesn't mean we're trying to stay here," she reminds us. "Some of it is what's put upon us. Some of it is the actions of others. Some fall down there and stay down there because of the simple fact that they don't know anything else."

SOME SOLUTIONS

Choncé Maddox Rhea is a freelance writer based out of Chicago, Illinois. Like Perry, she has also seen a great deal of poverty in her life.

"My family fell into poverty when my parents separated and my mom became a single mom," says Rhea. "She had her Certified Nurse's Assistant (CNA) license and worked a job making $11 per hour, but somehow still took care of my siblings and I. Money was always tight, and we lived on food stamps and received medical benefits for some time."

When Rhea was a sophomore in high school, her mother broke the news to her children that she could no longer afford their rent. They were going to have to move, but in order to do that she had to save up money for the new place.

Her mother and brother stayed with one of her nursing patients so she could rack up overtime as she was saving for the new apartment. Rhea and her sisters stayed at her uncle's house over the summer. She watched as her peers enjoyed the warm weather with friends and started their first jobs. Meanwhile, she was providing childcare for her sisters, enabling her mother to earn the money they so desperately needed to reestablish some stability.

A few years later, Rhea became a teen mom.

"I entered my own state of poverty since I wasn't able to provide financially for my son," she says. "I went to college and juggled part-time jobs but still relied on government benefits to help me get by as I worked on my education and developed more marketable skills."

These programs—combined with some serious hard work—helped Rhea get ahead in life. She used government programs, food pantries, clothes closets, nonprofit organizations, low-income housing, and sometimes even soup kitchens to get what she and her family needed as she strove towards the higher education which would allow her to propel herself to the next level.

Our society judges people severely when they utilize support programs or safety nets. This particularly bothers Perry as a woman of color because even the welfare system in our country has been racist since the beginning. When the New Deal was enacted, Social Security benefits were not extended to domestic and agricultural workers—who were primarily black at that time.[14] Once the system started becoming gradually more—but never close to completely—fair, white people started loudly complaining that they were supporting people of color, completely ignoring the fact that systemic poverty purposefully and disproportionately affects minorities.

"If we're on Medicaid and/or food stamps, we're trying to game the system. We're welfare queens," says Perry, citing the judgements welfare recipients commonly face—especially welfare recipients who are women of color. "Are there women who take advantage of these programs? Yes. Are they all women of color? No. For some of us, that's all we've got. Right now, I just moved up here [to Seattle] from Texas going on two months ago. [Perry moved for safety reasons.] For right now, I have a part-time job with Amazon. I don't get insurance there. My alternative is getting on Medicaid. Before I had a job, I got a food stamp card because I couldn't afford groceries during my job hunt."

Rhea encourages people to ignore these judgements, put their pride away, and seek out the same help she and Perry did. She encourages people to take advantage of every last resource and support so they can break the cycle of poverty, too.

PROGRAMS THAT CAN HELP

If you've never applied for benefits before, know that it's far from an easy process. Depending on the program you're applying for and your state, you'll need to provide proof of income for some months, data on all of your family members, bank statements, information about your monthly bills, and potentially information about any assets you may have, like a car or a house.

The next time someone tells you getting benefits is easy, check them on it!

It is worth it, though, if you can get on a program that will help you improve your station. Here are some US programs to look into:

- **SNAP.** *Formerly known as food stamps.*

- **Cash assistance.**

- **LIHEAP.** *This program helps with your heating bill in the winter.*

- **CAP Programs.** *These programs—which may be run by an outside agency rather than your state government—help control your electric bill.*

- **Childcare assistance.** *Typically this will be on your welfare application, but some states will refer you out to a third-party agency who facilitates the program after you've applied.*

- **Medicaid.** *Get on insurance. If you're having trouble because of your individual state's policies, be sure to look at the CHIP program—which is very low-cost and generally has higher* *income limits—to get your children covered so they can get the medical care they need.*

- **Pell and State grants.** *These are available by filling out the FAFSA form, and will help pay for a large chunk of your schooling.*

- **Special allowances.** *Some states offer special allowances for targeted life expenses. For example, Pennsylvania offers a special allowance for college textbooks for qualifying applicants.*

- **Section 8 Housing.** *These housing vouchers can help you get a roof over your head.*

- **Food pantries.** *Food pantries do not typically ask for proof of income, but their hours do tend to be limited. It's not like a store where you can just walk in. Some food pantries will even require that you set up an appointment or place your order before coming to pick it up.*

- **Soup kitchens.** *These are open to the public.*

- **Clothes closets.** *Some closets will help you get the basics, while others will help you put together a professional wardrobe so you can land that job.*

- **Local nonprofits.** *Look for nonprofits in your own community. They may offer job placement assistance, financial assistance, discounts on used vehicles, or even advocacy when you go to apply for benefits with your state's department of public welfare. If you have gaps, these nonprofits are often able to connect you with ways to fill them. Some examples that are generally available nationwide are the United Way, YWCA, and sometimes even Goodwill Industries.*

DON'T FORGET TO FACTOR IN HARD WORK

Being on welfare programs is no picnic. There are endless applications to fill out, income limits that seem to vary with every program, and the constant, though unwarranted, shame our society places on the "takers," as some crude and ignorant politicians describe benefit recipients.

These programs are exhausting, and they remind Rhea of another one of those prejudices that really gets under her skin.

"The one I really hate is when people complain about being tax payers and funding government programs for low-income families," she says. "Even when I was living below the poverty line, I still legally worked and paid taxes myself, so I didn't really get that argument. Plus, I know there are some people who are unable to work due to a disability or another hardship, so every situation is different. Low-income households shouldn't be generalized or judged."

But since reliance on welfare isn't a fun place to be, it's important to endure some growing pains and put in some serious hard work if you are able to do so. (Though as Rhea so rightly points out, not everyone can.)

To be able to pull off this great feat, you're going to have to dig deep to find your ultimate motivation. For Rhea, that drive came from two places. First, she was angry that she was stuck in this cycle, and she used that anger to fuel her forward motion. In contrast to her anger, she also fiercely loves her son. She wanted a better life for him, and that vision kept her pushing towards a better tomorrow even when things got incredibly difficult.

Jackie Cummings Koski is a sales executive at a global data company in Dayton, Ohio. She was raised by a single father who worked in a factory. He never applied for assistance programs, despite living well below the poverty level while raising six children.

"We would have done better if we were on welfare," Koski says. "For my dad, it was a sense of pride for some reason."

Koski worked her way through college, eventually establishing a good career for herself. Putting herself through school was a harrowing process, but she was driven by much the same motivation as Rhea: a better future for her own someday family.

AVOIDING DEBT

Koski attributes a large portion of her success to not taking on debt. She has never held credit card debt. She didn't take out any loans in school until her senior year, and even then the amount was minimal—just enough to help her get by.

"Looking back, the habit of not taking on debt or using a credit card to live on? It put me ahead while a lot of my colleagues and friends were paying off student loan debt. My money was going to investing and savings in my 401k."

Koski didn't use the Free Application for Financial Student Aid (FAFSA) to get grant money for college, but she does wish more people knew about it so they, too, could avoid student loans. Or even just be encouraged to get the education they need in the first place.

"I work with a lot of women of color in low-income communities," Koski relates. "They don't have a lot of money to work with. I share with them that going back to school doesn't cost a penny financially— it just takes a little bit of time. There are some people that have just kind of given up on the idea of college, but there's always a way."

To learn more about going to school for free when you're low-income, be sure to keep reading as we'll cover it in Chapter 4.

"Growing up, we knew when grocery day was because the fridge was empty with nothing in it," recounts Koski. "When you grow up like that, you can do two things. You can repeat what you know or do the opposite. In my head I wanted to do the opposite. It's fresh in your mind how it was—you never want to go back there and see it again. I wanted to change things for future generations."

Motivation, education, and hard work were all integral for all of the women I talked to, but Koski pointed out another factor that is fortunately becoming easier to control: your environment.

"We are products of our environment," she says. "When your household, community, city—everyone's in poverty, you never learn or do anything different. You have to somehow create a different environment for yourself."

While you might not be able to immediately change your physical environment, Koski notes that you do have a lot of control over your digital environment. You can educate yourself on financial matters more easily than at any time in the past, and you can find communities of like-minded people who have either already found their way out or who have concrete plans to escape the cycle of poverty.

If connecting via the written word isn't your thing, remember that there are lots of ways to consume content. Believe it or not, you can find YouTube channels, podcasts, and other mediums full of personal finance content—and it's not all dry and boring. In fact, a lot of it is actually pretty exciting once you've connected with a community from which you can learn.

DON'T LET HOPE DIE

Poverty is ridiculously difficult to escape. Everything is working against you. Banks charge more fees to clients who don't hold large enough minimum balances—if they'll give you a bank account at all. It's harder to keep your credit score up to qualify for advantageous rather than predatory financial products when there's no margin for error in your budget. Small inconveniences become major emergencies very quickly when you don't have as many resources at your disposal, and to top it all off, these financial struggles come with immense levels of stress, which further affect your ability to deal.

But there is hope. There are ways out. You can get a formal education if you don't already have one. You can educate yourself on financial topics through the power of the internet. If you focus your motivation on your efforts, the hard times will be easier to bear. And if you humble yourself, there are programs out there that will help you with food, heat, childcare, and more as you work to build yourself a better life.

There is no guarantee that your efforts will be rewarded. But if you don't make the decision to try, there's zero chance you're going to reach your dreams and goals. Fan the embers of hope, as you may be able to nurture them into a blazing fire for all those around you to see. After they've seen it, you can pass on the knowledge you've acquired and help them start their own fires, too.

TAKE ACTION 💲

- *Cut down your expenses as much as possible—though I recognize you likely have already.*

- *Read Chapter 4 to find out how to get a formal education for free if you don't already have one.*

- *Start reading at least one article a day on a financial topic you are interested in learning more about. (You could also consume one YouTube video, podcast episode, etc.) This will help you find community and support and change your digital environment.*

- *Figure out your "why." What is your ultimate motivation that will keep you going even when times get hard or the system tries to push you back down?*

- *Research and enroll in any programs that will help you access the resources you need—whether those resources are food, childcare, rent money, transportation, or cash.*

- *Know that times will get hard, but do everything you can to bolster your hope of better days ahead. The hope doesn't mean they will absolutely happen, but without that hope, you're sure to stay where you are or even slip further into poverty.*

- *If you find your own way out of poverty, reach out to your community and show them how you did it. Now that you have achieved, it's time to show everyone else that your hope was not unfounded and that they may be able to achieve their goals, too, despite "the man."*

PART TWO

EARN MORE

CHAPTER IV
Still I Rise

Getting an education as a nontraditional student.

I work in a field where outliers are celebrated, where you're told you don't *need* a college degree because there's that one guy who built his tech empire without one. Some even go as far as to argue that because a few people built multimillion-dollar businesses without a degree, pursuing higher education is a waste of money.

I'm genuinely happy for those who reach such great success without getting a degree. They have my upmost respect. They've worked hard and made something brilliant happen despite lacking formal higher education.

However, they are outliers.

In the fourth quarter of 2017, the difference between the median weekly income of an American woman with a high school diploma only versus someone with a bachelor's degree or higher was $514/week. That comes out to a difference of at least $2,056/month.[15]

It's a similar story in Canada. Women with a bachelor's degree earn 58 percent more than those with a high school diploma only. In a strange twist, women with apprenticeship certificates earned 12 percent *less* than those with only a high school diploma.[16]

The point is, pursuing a post-secondary degree is still a great investment. If you're living in or on the brink of poverty, returning to school has the potential to greatly increase your earning capabilities.

FINANCING SCHOOL AS AN AMERICAN

Even though college costs have ballooned significantly in the recent past, if you are a low- or middle-income adult, there's a high likelihood that you could go back to school for free. In fact, you may even be able to get paid to pursue an education.

That means no student loan debt. It means not stressing out over how you're going to pay for books.

It means you can do this.

CHOOSING A SCHOOL

There are several different types of colleges out there, and not all are priced equally. Keep an open mind about all of your options as you consider reentering the halls of scholarship.

COMMUNITY COLLEGE

Community college is typically the most affordable option. It's also the one likely to net you the most money. If you don't have a two-year degree yet, it's not a bad idea to start here. Credits are usually cheaper at community colleges than at four-year schools, and it's unlikely that you'll be the only adult learner in the classroom.

STATE SCHOOLS

If you go to community college first, you're likely going to want to head to a state school next. This is because state schools usually have agreements with community colleges guaranteeing credit transfer. That means you're less likely to have to repeat any courses you already took at the community college.

State schools are subsidized by state governments. This tends to make them cheaper than private institutions, although it should be noted that since the Great Recession, states have enacted austerity policies when it comes to state school funding. This means they've reduced how much money they invest in the state school system. These policies have played a large role in the rising cost of college tuition.[17]

Even with these changes in policies, state schools are still often the cheapest four-year schools for most students.

PRIVATE FOUR-YEAR INSTITUTIONS

Private colleges and universities are typically among the most expensive of all your options. They don't receive the same subsidies state schools do, and institutional aid isn't always prolific.

That doesn't necessarily mean a private school is off the table. You may be offered a great financial aid package or win a ton of scholarships that will cover tuition. But it does mean you need to go into the process with your eyes wide open to potential pricing differences.

Make sure your school is a nonprofit. We'll get to why in a minute.

IVY LEAGUE SCHOOLS

The likes of Cornell and Middlebury come with astronomical sticker prices. That doesn't mean they're out of reach.

Ivy league schools compete for the best students, and they want the best students whether they can afford tuition or not. To facilitate student acquisition, these institutions have sizeable endowments to cover those insane sticker prices for low- and middle- income students. Some schools will give you a full ride even if your income is in the low six-figure range.

If you get into one of these schools—and most do accept nontraditional and transfer students—you're less likely to end up with an unaffordable tuition bill than if you went to a non-Ivy private institution.

FOR-PROFIT FOUR-YEAR SCHOOLS

Be extremely wary of for-profit four-year institutions. The Consumer Financial Protection Bureau (CFPB) has sued many such colleges over the past several years. These schools tend to care less about whether you get a degree or come out of school competent enough to work in your field and more about the money they will make off of you as a student. You may find yourself being offered financing options through the school with terrible terms, and your grants and scholarships are unlikely to go as far as they would at the other four types of institutions.

It's also important to know that shady for-profit colleges will target lower-income students. They do this because they know you'll qualify for the maximum in grant awards after you fill out the FAFSA. They want the federal dollars you'll bring in, but don't always care as much about giving you a quality education.

THE FAFSA

The first step in your financial aid journey is filling out the Free Application for Federal Student Aid (FAFSA). You can find the application at: http://fafsa.ed.gov.

You don't have to know exactly where you'll be attending school to fill out the FAFSA. The most important thing is to fill it out as soon as possible. Applications open on October 1 of every year. So if you were applying for the 2020-21 school year, you would want to file your application as close to October 1, 2019, as you can.

Filling out the FAFSA used to be a tiring process that involved pulling out a hard copy of your tax return, but in recent years it's become far easier. Now the FAFSA simply pulls your tax and income data from the IRS. The tax information will be pulled for the year before the year in which you are filling out the FAFSA. That means if you're filling out the FAFSA in October of 2019 for the 2020-21 school year, the FAFSA will pull data from your 2018 tax return.

You will be asked if you want to enter your parents' income information. If you're age twenty-four or older, you are considered independent, meaning you can check the "no" box. Only *your* income will be counted. If you're under the age of twenty-four, you may qualify as an independent student if:

- *You're married.*

- *You're going for a master's or doctorate degree.*

- *You're currently on active duty serving in the US armed forces.*

- *You have children or will have children at the time you'll be going to school. You must be providing at least 50 percent of the support for these children.*

- *You have other dependents who receive at least 50 percent of their support from you.*

- *You're an orphan, were in foster care, or you were a dependent or ward of the court.*

- *You are or were an emancipated minor.*

- *Someone other than your parents had legal guardianship of you.*

- *You have been a homeless unaccompanied youth—or at risk of becoming homeless—at any point since July 1 of the year in which you are applying.*

If you don't meet any of those criteria, you're a dependent student—whether your parents do anything to support you or not.

There are several ways you may receive aid via the FAFSA. Let's delve into each one of them.

PELL GRANTS

Grants are money that you don't have to pay back. You'd only have to pay this money back if you don't keep your grades up.

The government issues grants based on your income. You may be surprised to learn that you can get Pell Grant funding even if you don't consider yourself "low-income." This is especially true if you have kids or other dependents.

We could get into the income formula here, but it's complex and not something with which you need to be familiar. What you do need to know is that almost every single year, the government has Pell Grant money left over. There is funding available; you just have to apply for it!

For the 2018-19 school year, a full Pell Grant is $5,920. Half will be paid during the first semester, while the other half will be disbursed at the beginning of the spring semester. Keep in mind that you can get a partial Pell Grant, too, depending on your financial standing and household size.

Here's where things get interesting: The average cost of tuition and fees at an average two-year public institution was $3,570 for the 2017-18 school year.[18] That means that if tuition stayed the same, students attending an average community college could pocket $1,175 from their Pell Grants *each semester* for books, housing, transportation, and food.

Yes, you can get paid to go to school. This is an especially viable route if you are lower-income.

If you decide community college isn't the right path for you, the average state school charged $9,970 in tuition and fees for the same school year. That means a full Pell Grant recipient would only need to drum up an additional $4,050 to cover the cost of attendance. And that's totally possible without digging into your own wallet.

FSEOG GRANTS

FSEOG grants are issued only to those in dire financial straits. However, if you do qualify, you can currently get anywhere between

$100 and $4,000 depending on your financial need. These grants do routinely run out of funding, which is a major reason why it's so important to file your FAFSA as close to October 1 as possible.

TEACH GRANTS

If you are planning on majoring in K-12 education, you may be eligible for a TEACH grant. TEACH grants are unique in that they come with a service obligation. In order to qualify, your college and your specific program must be associated with the TEACH program. You'll also have to keep your grades up.

When you accept this grant, you're agreeing that for at least four of your first eight years out of college, you'll teach a subject in a high-need field at a low-income school or educational service agency. You can learn more about current high-need fields at StudentAid.gov/TEACH.

If you fail to meet this service requirement, you'll have to repay the money plus interest.

If you meet all of these requirements, though, you can receive up to $4,000 in grant money every year.

IRAQ AND AFGHANISTAN SERVICE GRANT

If your parent or guardian died after 9/11 as the result of military service in Iraq or Afghanistan, you're eligible for this grant. The maximum award is the same as the Pell Grant. But this one isn't refundable. That means if you have financial aid in excess of your tuition, the Iraq and Afghanistan Service Grant will be reduced, and you won't be able to pocket any of the money for other expenses like food and shelter.

FEDERAL WORK-STUDY

You may be eligible for a job facilitated by your school. The job may be on or off campus, and in most positions you can decide whether you want your paycheck to go straight towards your tuition or if you'd like it to be deposited into your bank account.

FEDERAL STUDENT LOANS

There are several types of federal student loans, and those will be offered to you on the FAFSA as well. These loans are almost always preferable to private student loans from your bank or other financial institution.

But we're going to try to get you through school without debt, so we're not going to spend a lot of time here.

STATE GRANTS

After you complete your FAFSA application, you will likely be prompted to complete a financial aid application with your state. In my home state of Pennsylvania, income-based grants can be in excess of $3,000. That's another three grand for school that you *don't* have to pay back, or depending on your situation, another three grand you can keep for your living expenses.

If you're not immediately redirected to your state's financial aid application, search for your state's department of higher education. Call them directly to make sure you have everything you need to apply, but the application will most likely be online.

INSTITUTIONAL AID

You must fill out your FAFSA to even be considered for any financial aid from your college. If you qualify, you may be issued need-based grants. You may also be offered scholarships, which are another type of funding you don't have to pay back. Scholarships are typically merit-based but are sometimes included as a part of your financial aid package.

It's important to note that at some schools, your institutional aid will be reduced if you bring in money in excess of your tuition. For example, if you got a full Pell Grant plus a state grant of $3,000, you'd have $8,920 towards your tuition. The average state school costs $9,970. That means the maximum amount of institutional aid the school would offer you would be $1,050.

Let's say they offered you $1,050 and then you brought in an outside scholarship worth $1,000. The school would then reduce your institutional aid to $50. That means you can't pocket any of the money to help with your books or living expenses.

This is not an ideal situation, especially as a nontraditional student. You can find out if your school will allow you to keep money in excess of your tuition or if the school will reduce institutional aid by contacting the financial aid office before making your final decision about which college you want to attend.

SCHOLARSHIPS

If you're not immediately offered a scholarship right out of the gate, all is not lost. There are a ton of ways to get your hands on scholarship money. If the stipulations of the scholarship allow you to use the money for expenses outside of tuition, this can be a great source of money to help fund day-to-day expenses like rent and food while you're a student.

WHERE TO FIND SCHOLARSHIPS

Ashley Hill, a scholarship search strategist located outside of Atlanta, Georgia, says you should start your search at the hyperlocal level.

First, she says nontraditional students should check local colleges and universities—even if they don't plan on going to school locally. Some of the scholarships they offer may be exclusively for their students, but others—known as external or private scholarships—do not have an attendance requirement. Hill says that typically, the primary factor in eligibility is local residency.

Hill's next line of attack is your city or locality. She recommends checking your city government, nonprofits, and local chapters of any industry association linked to your desired major for any scholarship opportunities they may provide.

The third sphere Hill says you should check is your county. Your county government or organizations that serve your entire county may offer scholarship opportunities if you're willing to look for them.

Finally, check with your state. Just as many states offer grants, some may also offer scholarship opportunities. It's also a good idea to check with statewide organizations.

Besides scholarships based on your geographic location, Hill encourages nontraditional students to look to their employers for any scholarship opportunities that may exist. She says some employers also extend tuition reduction programs to their employees, saving students anywhere from 20 percent to 30 percent.

DO YOU HAVE WHAT IT TAKES?

Before you apply for a scholarship, it's helpful to know what the committee is looking for.

"At the heart of the essay, scholarship judges are looking for evidence of leadership experience, either through working or serving the community," says Hill, who judges scholarship competitions herself.

She notes that if you're a nontraditional student, you might not have the same amount of time on your hands as a teenager does to get out in the community and work on service projects. That doesn't mean you're an inferior candidate. Instead, you can draw upon your experiences in the workforce to demonstrate your leadership capabilities.

"Simply having a job and being on a team, working towards completing a project—it requires some leadership skills," says Hill.

"You don't have to be the manager or the president or the CEO to be a leader. You can lead right where you are."

WRITING YOUR ESSAY

The *pièce de résistance* of most scholarship applications is the essay. What is asked for will vary from application to application, but remember that what you need to showcase is those leadership skills and how you will use them to serve the community through your work in the future.

While you do want to use your essay to feature those skills, Hill cautions that it should not turn into a "brag list." You will be asked about your past academic performance and any awards you may have received on the scholarship application, so unless they are relevant to the story you're telling, they shouldn't appear in the essay.

She says that as you're writing the essay, you want to keep the prompt for the essay in mind. But you also want to be sure you're telling the panel a story that features your leadership skills and how you plan to apply them moving forward. Weaving the prompt and your personal story together is the key to success.

"It's not about the number of hours [in leadership positions] you have," she says, "but about the quality of those experiences."

FELLOWSHIPS

If you are going back to college to attend grad school, looking into fellowships can be worthwhile. Fellowships, like grants and scholarships, do not need to be repaid. They are issued to graduate students pursuing their master's or doctorate degrees and can bring in $50,000 or more to fund your research and living expenses. They do tend to be extremely competitive, and not all are in the five-figure range. That doesn't mean they're not worth pursuing.

To find relevant fellowships, Hill says you can start by googling "fellowship + (your major here)." Another great place to get more information is from the financial aid office of the school(s) you want to attend.

DOING THE MATH

Let's say you're going to a state school to complete an undergraduate degree. The tuition is $9,970 per year. You qualify for a full Pell Grant and a state grant of $3,000, bringing your total financial aid thus far to $8,920.

You're over the moon that you only owe $1,050 towards tuition, but you know you can do even better. You apply for refundable scholarships, being careful to read the terms and conditions on each application. Of the ten you apply for, you are awarded five. Each scholarship is worth $2,000 to be spread over two semesters. That means that partway through each semester, your school—which you know allows refundable scholarships because you checked before you applied—cuts you a check for $4,475.

It might not cover your living expenses for the entire semester, but $4,475 twice a year definitely reduces the number of hours you have to work, alleviating some of the stress of going back to school. If you want to eliminate work completely, it can be done. You just have to search and apply for and then be awarded more refundable financial aid.

You're not only going to college for free; you're getting paid to do it.

FINANCING SCHOOL AS A CANADIAN

The sticker price of university in Canada is lower than in the US, with undergrad degrees averaging $6,571CAD/year.[19] Because college attendance actually reduces median income for women, we will not be reviewing financing options for apprenticeship fields. We will only be looking at financing the cost of university.

FUNDING THROUGH THE GOVERNMENT OF CANADA

There are a few federal grants and programs that may help you fully fund school as a nontraditional student depending on your income, family situation, and province or territory of residency. Because they run their own financial aid programs at the provincial or territorial level, residents of the Northwest Territories, Nunavut, and Quebec are not eligible for the following grants from the Government of Canada.

To apply for these grants, you will need to contact the organization overseeing financial aid in your province or territory. Each province or territory has their own application process, but typically you only have to fill out one form to be considered for the following types of aid. Be sure to ask about the specifics in your area before filling out the application. To find out which organization you need to approach, check out the information for your province or territory on the Government of Canada website.

CANADA STUDENT GRANT FOR FULL-TIME STUDENTS

If you're enrolled in a full-time program of study, the Canada Student Grant for Full-Time Students can give you up to $3,000 per year as long as your school qualifies. Again, grants are money you don't have to pay back.

If you're single, you can currently get the full grant with a gross income of up to $30,000 CAD. But a prorated amount can still be awarded to you if your income is up to $61,513 CAD.

If you have three kids, or a partner and two kids, you can get the full grant with an income of up to $60,000 CAD. You can get a prorated award if your income is $112,817 CAD or less.

The income limits are liberal, going all the way up to $138,897 CAD for a family of seven.

Recently, this grant became even more attractive for nontraditional students. As of August 1, 2018, if you've been out of school for over

10 years, you are eligible for up to $1,600 CAD in additional funding each year, bringing the potential grand total to $4,600 CAD.[20]

If you qualify for this grant, you now only need an additional $1,971 CAD to cover tuition at your average university.

CANADA STUDENT GRANT FOR FULL-TIME STUDENTS WITH DEPENDENTS

If you have children, this grant could net you an additional $1,600 per school year for each dependent you have under the age of twelve. If you have a dependent over age twelve, they still count if they have a disability.

For this grant, you do have to qualify as a low-income household. These income thresholds vary based on your province or territory of residence. As an example, we'll look at Manitoba, which has the highest income threshold—and New Brunswick, which has the lowest.

A single mother of two children under the age of twelve in Manitoba can earn up to $38,143 CAD and still qualify for this grant. That same woman in New Brunswick could only earn up to $32,041 CAD. These numbers go up depending on the number of children you have, maxing out at $65,953 CAD for a family of seven in Manitoba.[21]

CANADA STUDENT GRANT FOR STUDENTS WITH PERMANENT DISABILITIES

If you have a permanent disability, whether it be physical or mental, you could qualify for this grant, which awards students $2,000 CAD per academic year. You will have to submit medical documentation in order to qualify.

If you need exceptional accommodations, you should also be aware of the Canada Student Grant for Services and Equipment for

Students with Disabilities, which gives you up to $8,000 CAD per year for these accommodations.

PROGRAMS FOR INDIGENOUS WOMEN

The federal government runs several programs for First Nations, Inuit, and Metis university students. The University and College Entrance Preparation Program funds one year of tuition, books, supplies, travel costs, and living expenses for a limited number of First Nations or Inuit students in an effort to increase the number of students prepared for post-secondary education.

The Post-Secondary Student Support Program provides up to $35,000 CAD per year for First Nations or Inuit undergrad students to fund their tuition, travel expenses, and living expenses while they are at school.

The Legal Studies for Aboriginal People Program provides support to Metis and Non-Status Indians as they enter the field of law. This program is administered by Indspire, an organization which also has numerous grant, scholarship, and bursary opportunities for indigenous students.

Finally, on the Government of Canada's website, you'll find the Indigenous Bursaries Search Tool, which can help you find even more money you won't have to pay back for your university education.

PROVINCIAL AND TERRITORIAL BURSARIES, GRANTS, AND SCHOLARSHIPS

Your province or territory may offer bursaries, grants, and scholarships. This is true in the Northwest Territories, Nunavut, and Quebec as well, where the provincial governments receive financial aid dollars from the federal government but do not participate in federal programs. Instead, all programs are run at the provincial or territorial level.

This funding source is typically available through the same application you fill out for federal aid. The process does vary from province to province and territory to territory, though, so it is best to check with the organization that manages financial aid in your area.

PRIVATE SCHOLARSHIPS

Private scholarships are available in Canada. To find them, you'll use much the same method as American students. Be sure to turn back a few pages to read Hill's advice under the "Scholarship" section for Americans.

TAKE ACTION $

American Students

- *Decide which school is right for you, keeping cost of attendance in mind.*

- *Look for and apply for scholarship opportunities ASAP.*

- *Look for and apply for fellowship opportunities if you are a grad student.*

- *Fill out the FAFSA.*

Canadian Students

- *Decide which school is right for you, keeping cost of attendance in mind.*

- *Look for and apply for private scholarship opportunities ASAP.*

- *Apply for grants, bursaries, and scholarships through the organization that manages financial aid in your province or territory.*

- *Indigenous students can check for additional grants, scholarships, and bursaries on the Government of Canada website and through Indspire.*

CHAPTER V
Hearth & Home

Twenty-three percent of American children are raised by single women.

The modern family is always changing. Gone are the days when our culture embraced traditional roles and structures at all costs. Today, a family can be a grandmother raising her grandchildren; two parents who both have children from previous relationships; or a couple who chooses not to have children at all.

These structures are many and diverse. But outside of the traditional nuclear family, no family structure is so prevalent as households led by single mothers. In 1960, 88 percent of American children lived with two parents. By 2016, that number had dropped to 69 percent. In the same time period, the number of children living with their mother only rose dramatically, from 8 percent to 23 percent.[22]

In Canada, where the culture tends to be a bit more progressive, the percentage of single-father households has risen at a much faster rate since the turn of the century when compared to single-mother households. But even with this surge in changing gender roles, single-mother households are still the norm for single-parent households, making up 80 percent of the demographic.[23]

This is a problem for women, because we tend to be economically disadvantaged. Whether that is a result of the wage gap, the investment gap, or any other factor, we tend to have less money and yet are more commonly responsible for economically and emotionally caring for a larger number of people.

Finding yourself in this situation raises quite a few conundrums. How are you supposed to work and care for your children? Childcare is insanely expensive, but you can't provide without spending a good portion of your hours bringing in an income.

What do you do when your kid gets sick, or when you need to take some time off to recover from childbirth?

How are you supposed to save for the future when you're the only one pulling in money—money that barely covers the present?

To find out how others have coped, I talked to some amazing women who have managed to thrive in their roles as single mothers, picking up some tips and tricks along the way.

CHILDCARE

In Chapter 3, we learned about Choncé Maddox Rhea's struggles with poverty. After her parents' divorce, she grew up in poverty, and she continued to have many of the same problems as a young adult after becoming a teen mom.

In the first couple years of her son's life, she received a lot of support from her mom as she worked hard to build a better life for herself and her child. For two years, she saved relentlessly until she finally had enough money to move out on her own. The move was sparked primarily by educational interests; Rhea had finished her associate degree and wanted to transfer to a four-year university.

> *Reminder: Find out how to go to school for free by flipping back to Chapter 4.*

"It was difficult studying, working, and paying all the bills and taking care of my son each day," says Rhea. "I was living about thirty to forty minutes from my mom and siblings, so while they could come out occasionally, I didn't really see them as often anymore. I definitely wasn't the average college student, with a two-year-old roommate, but thanks to campus childcare and a group of student parents who provided support, I was able to graduate two years later with my journalism degree."

Campus childcare was subsidized and free to Rhea. If you are a college student, too—or if you'd like to be—make sure to look into the CCAMPIS program. Under this program, the Department of Education provides funding to institutions of higher education so they can provide childcare to low-income student parents.

In the past couple of years, you may have heard some scary things about the CCAMPIS program. In its 2018 budget proposal, the Trump administration wanted to take away all of its funding. That didn't go over well, so the 2019 proposal included funding, but kept it at the same rate—which is a problem, because there are more student parents than ever. Many of these programs have a waiting list because they are already unable to provide adequate services to all of their students with the funding currently available.

The good news is that a president's budget proposal is just that: a proposal. Congress controls the budget, and as a part of the 2018 spending package they passed earlier this year, funding for the CCAMPIS program actually went up from $15 million to $50 million. That being said, the Department of Education is an arm of the executive branch, so we'll have to cross our fingers and hope nothing crazy happens with that funding. After all, we live in a world where even the unthinkable has suddenly become possible.

If your school doesn't have a CCAMPIS program or the waiting list at your school is too long, not all is lost. Rhea recommends getting in touch with your local Department of Human Services to find information about childcare benefits. These benefits pay for a portion or all of your childcare expenses whether you're a student or working mother. Some states may have employment requirements, but your caseworker should be able to help you sort out the specifics.

In my experience, the level of helpfulness your local welfare department will provide is highly dependent on where you live. I've lived some places where these offices were extremely helpful to their clientele, pointing out additional programs that could help them about which the clients were previously unaware. I've also lived places where the person at the front desk seemed to get paid to get people to turn around and walk out the door before speaking to anyone. These same offices had social workers who conveniently "didn't see" supporting documents that had been uploaded into the system and denied disabled children health care benefits because of it, resulting in a delay of access to vital medical care.

It's a mixed bag out there. If you live in one of the areas with not-so-great customer service, look around your community for nonprofit organizations that advocate on behalf of welfare recipients. They'll be able to connect you with programs that you and your child need, including health care—which should be available to your child via CHIP regardless of income level.

Of course, they'll also be able to help you with any childcare programs that may exist. I've seen the YWCA running these programs in some parts of the country, and the United Way is one national nonprofit that can help you figure out the application process. If you're frustrated with your welfare office and are having problems locating a local nonprofit on your own, these two organizations are a good place to start your search.

Rhea graduated in two years with a degree in journalism, but she couldn't have done it without help from her family, the support of other student parents, and subsidized childcare. Lean on your family if you can. Seek out other student or working parents and ask for a helping hand, keeping in mind that it's appropriate to return the favor whenever possible. And make sure you go through though government- or school-sponsored programs to get your child the care they need while you get the job you need so you can provide for them.

IT'S THEIR CHILD, TOO.

When it comes to child support, know that asking for it is not greedy. It does not make you any less independent. If there's any way possible for you to pursue that money for your child, do it.

"You should make sure you are getting the child support your child deserves," says Jackie Cummings Koski, who is a sales executive at a global data company, a single mother, and the child of a single father. "Some women seem to not want to pursue that. I have a lot of African-American friends not going through the court system to get the support. But the money's not for you—it's for the child. And the child deserves support from both parents."

CARETAKER AND BREAD EARNER

Being both the primary caretaker and the primary bread earner is a heavy task that requires some sacrifices. Jackie Cummings Koski was very secure in her career both before and after her divorce left her a single mother. Yet there were opportunities she knew she couldn't pursue because of her status as a single mom.

Because she was the custodial parent, she didn't feel comfortable looking at positions that required travel. No regrets—she wanted to be there for her daughter and built a good career for herself without being required to hop on a plane every other week. But Koski's experiences do highlight the fact that many single parents have to make career sacrifices. Taking that big promotion that comes with added time at the office or out of town just may not be possible.

If you're not in the same career position Koski was, you may have even more basic concerns. What do you do about maternity leave, for example? While the Family Medical Leave Act (FMLA) does provide for twelve weeks unpaid leave for American mothers, 44 percent of working moms do not qualify for various reasons.[24] Maybe their employer isn't large enough to be bound by this law. Maybe they aren't scheduled for enough hours to be eligible for the protections the FMLA provides.

Whatever the individual reasons, these women are left in a financial quagmire. Assuming you're paid hourly, you'll be missing out on your pay while you're giving birth and recovering. On top of that, if you don't qualify for FMLA leave, you also run the real risk of losing your job permanently. Do you return to work before you are fully recovered, or do you take the time your body needs to recover and lose your primary source of income?

One way to combat this problem is to take out a short-term disability policy if you're a woman in your childbearing years. These policies pay you a percentage of your normal income—typically for six to eight weeks. They don't solve the problem of holding onto your job if you don't qualify for FMLA leave, but they do provide you with income to get by during those weeks when you need to be giving your body time to heal.

It's important to note that most insurers will not cover pregnancy or childbirth if you make a claim within nine to twelve months of opening your policy. That means it's important to get one of these policies prior to conceiving—even if you don't think you're going to have kids. Life can take us by surprise sometimes, so it's best to be prepared.

Many employers will bring in a third-party insurer to sell these policies at least once a year. If they're not bringing in an insurance rep, you can directly ask your supervisor or HR department if your company works with a specific insurance company to provide this benefit. You will have to pay a monthly premium, but it's typically worth the cost—especially since short-term disability can cover other unexpected emergencies like accidents or illnesses.

Some states even provide short-term disability benefits as a right. As of this writing, here are the places where you're able to claim partial pay if you're out due to childbirth or other types of short-term disabilities:

- **California.** *The state Disability Insurance program provides for 60 percent to 70 percent of your pay for up to fifty-two weeks—though there will need to be medical justification for the duration of your leave. If you do have a partner, they may also be able to use the Paid Family Leave program to get the same benefits for up to six weeks, allowing them to help care for and bond with your child as well. (www.edd.ca.gov/Disability/)*

- **Washington, D.C.** *Starting in July of 2020, Washington, D.C. will be providing Paid Family Leave. You'll get up to eight weeks to bond with your new child and up to two weeks to deal with your own health conditions. Maximum benefits will be $1,000/week. You can check out what yours will look like using the District of Columbia's calculator on the following information page. (https://does.dc.gov/page/district-columbia-paid-family-leave)*

- **Hawaii.** *Depending on what you do for work, you may be eligible for Hawaii's Temporary Disability Insurance program. If you qualify, you're eligible for up to twenty-six weeks of leave—as long as your leave period is certified as medically necessary by a health care professional. You will receive at least 58 percent of your normal take-home pay during this time period, with a maximum weekly benefit of $620/week in 2018. (labor.hawaii.gov/dcd/frequently-asked-questions/tdi/)*

- **New Jersey.** *You will be able to claim disability for as long as your doctor says is medically necessary—up to 26 weeks. During this time period, you'll get two-thirds of your normal pay up to $637/week in 2018. You (and your partner) are also entitled to six weeks of leave for bonding after the birth or adoption of a new child. The family leave pay structure operates in the same way as the temporary disability pay. (https://www.nj.gov/labor/tdi/tdihome.html)*

- **New York.** *You can claim disability for up to 26 weeks with the certification of a medical professional and will be compensated 50 percent of your pay. The kicker here is that the maximum benefit hasn't been changed since the 1980s, so it maxes out at $170/week— which for many women will be less than that 50 percent rate, anyway. However, New York state just started paying out benefits for Paid Family Leave in 2018. Here you can claim up to 50% of your pay with a maximum weekly benefit of $692.56 in 2018. The percentage will increase until 2021, when it will stabilize at 67 percent of your pay. If you have a partner, they can also use Paid Family Leave. The maximum benefit period is currently eight weeks but will progressively increase to 12 weeks by 2021. (https://www.ny.gov/new-york-state-paid-family-leave/paid-family-leave-information-employees)*

- **Puerto Rico.** *You can claim up to 26 weeks of disability under the SINOT program. Minimum benefits are $12/week, with the maximum ranging from $55/week to $113/week depending on your field. (http://trabajo.pr.gov/sinot.asp)*

- **Rhode Island.** *You can claim up to 30 weeks of disability under Rhode Island's plan with the endorsement of your doctor. Most new moms will probably not get the full 30 weeks, though. Maximum benefits are currently $837/week and are based on your income. The same payout is available for four weeks for caregiving and bonding. (http://www.dlt.ri.gov/tdi/)*

If you are not eligible for short-term disability through work or your state, you can look for plans on your own. Keep in mind, though, that it might make more financial sense to purchase a long-term disability plan, depending on the terms. Some plans will cover things like recovery from childbirth on top of covering anything that renders you incapable of working for the rest of your career. Be sure to compare both short-term and long-term products with an insurance agent you trust—ideally across multiple insurers.

Maternity leave options are far more generous in Canada. You can take both maternity and parental leave and receive up to 55 percent of your pay. Maternity leave caps out at 15 weeks, and parental leave at 35. If you want to extend your parental leave to 61 weeks, you can do so, but your benefits will be cut from 55 percent to 33 percent of your normal pay.[25]

Quebec has its own program. Maternity leave can either be 15 weeks with 75 percent of your pay, or 18 weeks with 70 percent of your pay. Parental leave can range from seven to 25 weeks with 55 to 75 percent of your pay.[26]

Self-employed Canadians should look at enrolling in the Employment Insurance program. If you're paying into it, you'll be able to reap benefits as well—even though you're not working for a traditional employer.

Finding a way to get through maternity leave is one thing, but your responsibilities don't end after the first year of your child's life. Single parents in particular face a daunting challenge when a child is home sick, an IEP meeting must be attended, or your child just wants you to be there to see them perform in the school play.

In most areas, you're up against a rock and a hard place. You'll have to find someone to cover your shift, use paid leave time, or hope your boss doesn't fire you for calling off work. However, some local governments are working to alleviate this burden by building in parental leave that extends beyond the infancy of your child. These American states have policies that will help:

- **California.** *Up to 40 unpaid hours off per year for your child's educational activities or childcare emergencies. You must use any paid or unpaid time off benefits before utilizing these 40 hours, which are protected by state law. (http://leginfo.legislature.ca.gov/faces/codes_displaySection.xhtml?lawCode=LAB&sectionNum=230.8)*

- **Illinois.** *Up to 8 unpaid hours off per year for your child's educational activities. You must use any paid time off first—but you can leave your sick days and disability leave intact. You also have a right to make up any hours you missed should you so wish. (http://www.ilga.gov/legislation/ilcs/ilcs3.asp?ActID=2409&ChapterID=68)*

- **Louisiana.** *This state's law is a bit wishy-washy, but it's encouraging that it exists at all. Your employer can choose to grant you 16 hours per year for school- or daycare-related events, but there's no penalty if they don't. (http://legis.la.gov/legis/Law.aspx?d=83324)*

- **Massachusetts.** *Up to 24 unpaid hours off per year for your child's educational activities or doctor's appointments. This is known as Small Necessities Leave. (https://www.mass.gov/guides/breaks-and-time-off)*

- **Minnesota.** *Up to 16 unpaid hours off per year for your child's educational activities; these hours cannot be scheduled outside of work hours. This applies to child care centers as well as K-12 education. You can use paid time off in lieu of these hours, but unlike other states, you are not required to use your paid time off before utilizing this benefit. (https://www.revisor.mn.gov/statutes/cite/181.9412)*

- **Nevada.** *Up to 4 unpaid hours off per year for your child's educational activities. Nevada's law specifies that you can use these hours to volunteer at class parties and other similar events. (https://www.leg.state.nv.us/NRS/NRS-392.html#NRS392Sec4577)*

- **North Carolina.** *Up to 4 unpaid hours off per year for your child's educational activities. Keep in mind that it's 4 hours per calendar year, and that you don't get extra hours if you have more than one child. (https://hr.duke.edu/policies/time-away/leave-parent-involvement-schools)*

- **Vermont.** *Up to 4 unpaid hours off per month for your child's doctor's appointments, educational activities, or medical emergencies. You can take up to 24 hours per year. (https://legislature.vermont.gov/statutes/section/21/005/00472a)*

- **Washington, DC.** *DC also gives 24 unpaid hours per year, and they even allow you to use it for things like soccer games. There is a hitch, though: your employer can deny your request for time off if they decide you not being there would put a significant damper on business operations. (https://code.dccouncil.us/dc/council/code/titles/32/chapters/12/)*

In Canada, these leave policies are executed provincially.

- **Alberta.** *Up to five unpaid days per year to attend to your family responsibilities. (https://www.alberta.ca/personal-family-responsibility-leave.aspx#toc-3)*

- **British Columbia.** *Up to five unpaid days per year. You can only use these days for events that relate to the care, health, or education of your child—things like field trips don't count. (https://www2.gov.bc.ca/gov/content/employment-business/employment-standards-advice/employment-standards/igm/esa-part-6-section-52)*

- **Manitoba.** *Up to three unpaid days per year. Manitoba is liberal in their definition of the scope of family leave—as long as it relates to "family responsibilities," you'll probably be okay. (https://www.gov.mb.ca/labour/standards/doc,family-leave,factsheet.html#q62)*

- **New Brunswick.** *Up to three unpaid days per year to attend to the care, education, or health of your child or another family member. (http://www2.gnb.ca/ content/dam/gnb/Departments/petl-epft/PDF/es/ FactSheets/OtherLeaves.pdf)*

- **Newfoundland & Labrador.** *Up to seven days unpaid leave per year. You will have to explain in writing the reason for your absence before taking time off. (http://www.aesl.gov.nl.ca/publications/labour/ labour_relations_work.pdf)*

- **Ontario.** *In Ontario, you cannot take time off work for school events, but you can to care for a sick or injured child under Personal Emergency Leave. You get up to 10 days per year. For the first two, you will continue to receive pay, though the last eight will be unpaid. (https:// www.labour.gov.on.ca/english/es/faqs/general.php#sick)*

- **Prince Edward Island.** *Up to three unpaid days per year to take care of family responsibilities. (https://www.princeedwardisland.ca/en/information/ workforce-and-advanced-learning/family-leave)*

- **Quebec.** *Up to 10 unpaid days per year. You can only use these days for events that relate to the care, health, or education of your child. (https:// www.educaloi.qc.ca/en/capsules/time-work-personal-and- family-reasons)*

You'll likely come up against all kinds of other challenges along your journey as you raise your child on your own. Maybe you wouldn't mind the additional emotional and economic support that comes with having a partner, but dating is hard even without kids in the mix. There will doubtless be scheduling conflicts when it comes to your job and your children's extracurriculars, and there will be some days when you don't know if you can take the constant hustle for one more second.

As you meet those challenges, first, know that you're not alone. There are so many other women going through the exact same thing. Reach out. Connect. Also know that as harried as you may feel, you are beautiful and strong. You are proving that strength every single day.

"Believe it or not, I actually embraced the challenge of being able to find my own independence," says Rhea, speaking of her six years as a single mother. "Yes, some days are difficult, but I have loved being a mom through it all. Even though I'm married now, I still have that grit and sense of independence that I developed when I was a single mom."

TAKE ACTION $

- *If you are returning to school, talk to someone at admissions or the student life office about free childcare services. This program may or may not be funded through CCAMPIS.*

- *If you are not a student, or if your school does not provide subsidized childcare, fill out an application with your local Department of Public Welfare. Apply for all benefits that may help you, but keep your eyes especially keen for childcare benefits.*

- *If you are of childbearing years, look into getting a short- or long-term disability policy. You can start your search through your employer. If your employer does not work with an agency that provides these benefits, start searching on your own through a trusted, independent insurance agent who will get you quotes across multiple insurance providers.*

- *Look into your state or province's short-term disability and/ or maternity leave policies. These benefits may already be available to you without an additional premium—if you live in the right area.*

- *Look into your state or province's leave policies for parents— specifically as they apply to protected time off for a child's illness, school events, or general education.*

CHAPTER VI
Just Because I'm Different Doesn't Mean I'm Scary

The effects of disablism are far-reaching and harmful to all of society.

You may not be familiar with the term disablism. Quite honestly, if disability hadn't impacted the lives of my loved ones, I wouldn't know what it was either.

In fact, we can deconstruct disablism within that simple statement. Disability—which I say has impacted my loved ones—to most abled people means "un"-able. There is something "wrong" with your body or mind that makes it so you can't function without accommodations.

Heather Watkins, a disability advocate from Boston, points out a very important aspect of the etymology of this word, though: "dis" doesn't only mean "the opposite of." In fact, this root is traditionally traced back to Latin, where it meant "twice" or was synonymous with the prefix "bi."[27] For this reason, Watkins chooses to evaluate her disability as her having another way—a second way—of being able to get things done. She isn't incapable; she is just another reflection of the duality of ability.

And that's where disablism comes in. The society we live in is built for neurotypical, "able"-bodied individuals. Very often, this same society gets its feathers ruffled when an accommodation is requested or even mandated by law. Why should the abled have to inconvenience themselves because of someone else's needs? Or if you look at it through a 'helper' mindset: Aren't I such a good person for helping this poor, incapable human being?

Either way, there is no empowerment. There is no acknowledgment of the fact that those with disabilities are an important part of our society. And there is no recognition that by failing to accommodate, we are hurting everyone—disabled or not.

Let's look at small businesses as an example. Sometimes, businesses dislike the fact that they have to comply with the Americans with Disabilities Act (ADA) by providing ramps, caring for sidewalks, hiring interpreters, and investing money in various ways that will help democratize access to their business. In fact, there have been several amendments proposed to the ADA since 2016 which contend that the nearly-thirty-year-old bill hasn't given a realistic path for small businesses to comply with the law. These proposals have led to significant protests from the disability community, including groups like ADAPT.

At this point, the ADA is older than some millennials. If you haven't built the cost of meeting accommodations into your budget, you don't have a viable business plan.

Watkins points out that by not providing accommodations, you are shutting out potential patrons. She notes that if there's not a ramp to your business, those with mobility issues aren't going to be able to spend money at your store or dine at your restaurant. Neither will their friends or family members. Instead, they'll take their cash elsewhere.

So disablism is pitying the disabled or looking at them as an inconvenience. You can exercise disablism intentionally or not, but once you're aware of it, you can start to modify your opinions and behaviors.

Allow me to be the first. That sentence in the first paragraph? I'm going to edit it:

> Quite honestly, if ~~disability~~ disablism hadn't impacted the lives of my loved ones, I wouldn't know what it was, either.

You see, being Autistic or Deaf doesn't inherently make life more of a struggle. In fact, these different ways of processing the world can add so much beauty to the human experience. The systems we have in place—the disablist systems that serve only a portion of the population—are what make life and finances so hard when you have a disability.

BRINGING IN AN INCOME

A major problem with our system is that it limits the income of the disabled, creating a type of forced poverty. If you're disabled, health care is of the upmost importance. While some states and provinces are extremely good at providing health care to the disabled regardless of age, others are not. For example, a disabled child can get onto Medicaid in Pennsylvania regardless of the amount of income the child's parents earn. Depending on the disability, the same is not necessarily true in other states, such as Utah. If you live with type 2 diabetes and have only provincial health care, you're going to be paying far more out of pocket if you live in New Brunswick than the Yukon, and in New Brunswick, your income will affect the amount of your coverage.

This leaves many individuals and families having to seriously assess if working more or working for a higher salary is going to negatively impact their health care coverage. Another area they have to worry about is disability benefits. In the US, some individuals get SSDI, where they get a monthly stipend because they have put so many years in at work before becoming unable to continue their careers. Others, however, receive SSI because their disability and disablism have prevented them from logging enough income to claim SSDI. SSI payments—which are well under $1,000/month at the maximum—require you not only to have a stunted income, but also to not have any significant assets built up.

A recent solution has come on the scene to combat asset tests, though. The solution is called an ABLE account. These accounts allow you to set aside up to $15,000 per year in an investment account, which can range anywhere from super aggressive and risky investments to a simple savings account that won't lose value. This savings is protected from Federal asset tests, and you can use the money for virtually anything that relates to the disabled person's life, including education and home or vehicle modifications, but also simple things like rent.

ABLE accounts are a major step in the right direction, but they don't solve the problem of income limitations. We're essentially forcing the disabled to work less so they won't lose the benefits they need to get by.

Aside from programs that directly affect the finances of the disabled, cultural systems and beliefs can play a large role in income, too. You might not get hired for a job because your need for accommodations is obvious to the employer. They'd never say that, because it would be illegal to do so. But they can say, "You just weren't the best fit. We're going with another candidate."

This cultural stigma can be internalized, too. Abigail Perry, a home-based customer service rep and the author of *Frugality for Depressives*, has had chronic fatigue since contracting Guillain-Barre Syndrome at age 19. The neurological illness has been resolved, but the fatigue remains. She has also been diagnosed with bipolar II disorder.

For a long time, the disablism that wreaked havoc on Perry was internalized.

"I didn't realize the financial implications of the fatigue at first because I was in denial, thinking I could somehow push through the exhaustion and work a regular job," recounts Perry. "But it soon became apparent that I couldn't handle a full-time job. Then I spent a few years scrambling to make ends meet via an assortment of part-time jobs, which were usually also more than I could handle.

"When I finally accepted that I needed to go on disability, I had just lost my job and had to move in with my mother, who then had to cover both of our expenses while she herself wasn't working, having just fled an abusive marriage. I spent the next two years waiting for disability, trying not to be too big a financial burden on my mom while I received $330 from the state.

"I'm an overachiever, so it was hell to be saddled with this condition that kept me from holding down a regular job. I hated my limitations, and I hated myself for having them. It took me a long time to say that I had a disability without qualifying it in an almost apologetic way. Because it was invisible to the naked eye, I was sure everyone doubted me—that they figured I just wasn't trying hard enough."

SAVING & BUDGETING

We've already discussed the rise of ABLE accounts and what a good thing they are for those who are trying to avoid federal asset tests. While not all states offer them, many of the states that do will allow you to participate in their plan without residency requirements.

Things start to get sticky after that, though. While you will be exempt from *federal* asset tests, your state can still technically impose their own asset tests on you for certain benefits—even if your savings are stashed in an ABLE account. This can be a major problem when you depend on some of those benefits to make it through your day-to-day life. Some states, like Pennsylvania, bar savings in an ABLE account from being counted against state health or disability benefits. All states need to follow this example by extending further protections under these plans that will protect disabled citizens regardless of their state of residence.

Watkins, who has had muscular dystrophy since birth, has a lot of interdependence in her family dynamic. She is caretaker to her father—who has a hidden disability—and mother to a young adult. While she tries to take care of everyone's needs, she has to be mindful that her budget is limited.

"You're always concerned," she says. "You have to make sure you're not going above income limits. It would affect my Medicaid in this state. I always have a running checklist in my mind to make sure I'm balancing everything—that includes my finances. I make sure I'm not spending too much so we can eat, keep the lights on, [and] pay car insurance and little things like that on a fixed budget."

On top of worrying about her Medicaid coverage, Watkins is also eligible for the Department of Education's Total and Permanent Disability Discharge program for her student loans. In order to qualify for discharge, she must live below the federal poverty line for a family of two for three years. This income limit is the same for everyone regardless of actual family size, though you won't have to go through this three-year monitoring period if your disability is certified by Veterans Affairs and was related to your service.

Watkins is strong and savvy and finds ways to get by. But this forced poverty is taxing. It makes budgeting harder as your income must be limited. When you have a limited income, finding the money to stash away into savings becomes that much harder; even if you have an ABLE account, you may not be able to fund it.

Perry notes that invisible disabilities can have a major effect on how you budget, too. With bipolar II, she experiences both depressive episodes and manias—though these euphoric experiences are far less extreme than those experienced by people with bipolar I. Mania can often lead to increased spending—sometimes dramatically so. Perry says that since her manic experiences are less acute, the largest splurge she's made during an episode was somewhere around $100.

The depressive episodes, however, have had a bigger impact on her budgeting and savings habits.

"Depression may make you want to buy things for comfort, or you may simply be too depressed to avoid the convenience tax," she explains. "For example, you might not be able to bring yourself to cook, so you get food delivered. You might not feel up to going to the supermarket and can only make it to the drug store, so you pay a premium for some food items."

For this reason, Perry and her husband leave their budget open-ended. They track and limit their overall spending but try not to self-blame if they end up spending more on specific line items when they 'could have' exercised more frugality.

"Depressives are going to be more likely to beat themselves up for not being able to follow a budget perfectly," says Perry, "and depending on the condition, people with [other] disabilities may find themselves in a similar situation. So I always recommend choosing a looser and/or more flexible budget. Build in some padding against the likely event that you won't be able to do things perfectly."

To do this on a limited budget, Perry notes that you're really going to have to drill down and figure out what you value most. Because no one can afford everything—and those on a limited budget can afford even less—you're going to have to make some hard decisions about what you will and won't spend money on as you prioritize each purchase's importance in your life. We should all do this, but it's especially important when you know your income is capped and exercising extreme frugality won't always be realistic.

SPENDING: MONEY AND EMOTIONAL CAPITAL

For Watkins, spending isn't just about fiscal capital. It's also about emotional capital and paying attention to where she spends her energy.

"I allot so much for paying the bills and making sure we have enough to eat," she says. She does something similar with her time. "I also look for areas where I can conserve energy because I don't know when I will need it later on in the day."

As she looks at where she spends her money and time as a disabled woman, she sees technology as a lifesaver. She uses PayPal to invoice and send money. She utilizes online banking to pay her bills. Spending a little more on grocery delivery services via apps is worth it for her, as it frees her to use her energy on other necessary tasks throughout the day. Doctor appointments are scheduled and reminders ping her throughout the day—all facilitated by the internet.

Watkins relies on her Wi-Fi connection to manage her spending. By doing this intentionally, she is able to spend her dollars where they matter most, just like Perry—even if that means spending a little more on a grocery service so she can have the energy she needs to cook at home or handle an important insurance claim later in the day.

But remember the forced poverty aspect of disablism? When you're living in poverty and looking for bills to cut, the internet can creep up to the top of the list as a nonessential. It's not as important as food, rent, or health care. But it's such an important tool with such a huge potential impact for disabled people that it's just plain wrong that someone would have to cross it off their budget because of the fixed income situation they've been forced into by the disablist system.

Fortunately, some internet carriers do have plans dedicated to low-income households. If you're thinking about nixing your service, reconsider. Contact your internet provider—or call all the potential internet providers in your area—and ask them for an application for their low-income household program. Your monthly bill with a lot of these carriers could end up being somewhere around $0 to $10.

EMPOWERMENT

As we examine all the negative financial effects of disablism, let's not forget that it's the system and not disability itself that causes these issues. Disabled people have a lot to contribute to our society at large, and neither pity nor stigma are viable solutions.

"I think the two worst kinds of 'help' are blind encouragement and inspiration porn," says Perry. "By 'blind encouragement,' I'm referring to the situations where people keep insisting that you can surpass your limitations; that they believe in you, and they're sure you can find a way to work if you just keep at it. As though you haven't tried everything you can think of to avoid going on disability, to stay a 'contributing' member of society. Because, yes, my disablism was so internalized that I felt like I had no value if I couldn't work—that I was simply a drain.

"Inspiration porn is an offshoot of blind optimism. People see all the feel-good stories on TV news and in movies of disabled people overcoming their conditions to achieve great things. They then expect all disabled people to be able to surpass limitations. And to be cheerful—nay, optimistic—about the whole thing. If we fail to be as plucky as expected, we may be told that our attitude is the problem and that we just need to think more positively and try a little harder. It's infuriating and exhausting—and perhaps worst of all, it makes most of us at least briefly doubt ourselves."

Watkins points out that those feel-good stories tend to focus on people succeeding *in spite of* their disability when really, nothing could be further from the truth.

"It's not 'in spite of.' It's 'because of.' I take my disability everywhere I go. It's factored into critical decision-making and quality of life decisions like housing, health care, where you work, accommodations, and parenting. You carefully consider all of your life's choices when you have a disability.

"It affects how I see and govern my life. It shapes my self-awareness. When I started reaching out via advocacy work, I was getting that mirrored back from other people with various disabilities. They were out-and-about, empowered advocates. That was a strong message to me. You have a disability and you're living your life in a comprehensive way—not through the lens of limitation only.

"We need to see the comprehensive view of what disability looks like on different bodies because strength and leadership looks different on different bodies. My disability has caused me to parent mindfully. It's why I show moral support to others—like ADAPT—out there protesting. I'm standing up sans apology in the world. You don't leave your disability behind—you take it with you. It is not a hurdle.

"My biology has informed my biography."

TAKE ACTION 💲

- *Look into ABLE plans to see if opening one might benefit you. Start with your own state, as this is where you're most likely—though not guaranteed—to get state tax benefits. If your state doesn't have an ABLE account option or if your state's investment options aren't your favorite, don't forget that you can look to other states' ABLE plans in many cases.*

- *Create a flexible budget, reminding yourself to not feel guilty over spending money on apps or services that help you conserve that emotional, mental, or physical energy. Many of these apps are free, but if you have to shell out a couple dollars a month for something that's going to make your life better, find another place in your budget to cut that amount that's not as big of a priority.*

- *Looking through the lens of empowerment so powerfully demonstrated by Watkins, examine your own feelings about disablism and any prejudices you may hold—whether they be internalized or born out of a lack of lived experience and inherited prejudices. Challenge these feelings within yourself, even if you initially feel uncomfortable.*

CHAPTER VII

The Elephant in the Womb

The gender pay gap.

I don't know if you've heard, but women get paid less than men—significantly less. And not all women suffer equally. In fact, the gender wage gap is a clear indicator that pay discrepancies are worse along racial and ethnic lines. Here's some hard data from the Spring 2018 Edition of the American Association of University Women's *The Simple Truth About the Gender Pay Gap:*

For Every $1 White Non-Hispanic Men Make, I Get Paid...

Asian $0.87	Native Hawaiian/ Pacific Islander $0.59
White (Non-Hispanic) $0.79	American Indian or Alaska Native $0.57
Black $0.63	Latina/Hispanic $0.54

On top of oppression based on race, transgender women face a 32 percent pay decrease after transition.[28]

When we look to our neighbors to the north, The Conference Board of Canada[29] measures pay gaps by race and gender—both across different provinces and for the nation as a whole. We know that a little less than one-third of visible minorities in Canada are born there, and that the country as a whole has a racial wage gap of 12.6 percent between visible minorities and Caucasians. This gap covers all university-educated, full-time workers born in Canada.

When we look at the racial wage gap for only women, we're comparing visible minority women to Caucasian women. Quebec has the largest gap at 20 percent, and Prince Edward Island has a reverse gap of -12.3 percent, which means that visible minority women in the province make 12.3 percent more than their Caucasian counterparts. The only other province that has this reverse trend for women is New Brunswick.

The national racial wage gap for all genders can be broken down further by ethnicity. Canada looks at this in far more depth than the data available for the United States:

Ethnicity	Wage Gap compared to Caucasian Canadians
Japanese	-3.6%
Chinese	7.7%
Korean	11.6%
South Asian	12.7%
Arab	13.0%
Southeast Asian	13.1%
Minorities not included elsewhere on the list	17.6%
West Asian	18.0%
Multiple visible minorities	18.9%
Black	19.6%
Filipino	20.5%
Latin American	31.7%

If you look at the immigrant population, there is a 7 percent pay gap between Canadian immigrants and Canadian-born workers. There is also an 11 percent gap between what Aboriginal women and non-Aboriginal women earn.[30]

Joyce Zahariadis was at her company for fifteen years before leaving to be the full-time caretaker of her Autistic children. She recounts her experiences as a Latina woman facing the biggest gender pay gap in America.

"As a Latina manager, I was seen as bitchy or needing to smile more so I didn't 'look bitchy,'" Zahariadis remembers. "Crying or being emotional wasn't allowed. When my coworkers saw me move up, it wasn't because I was good in their minds. It was because 'they needed a Latina.'"

All this is to say that in both the United States and Canada, we have a long way to go as far as eradicating sexism, racism, and ethnocentrism in the workplace goes. We have the data. We know these gaps are real. Much like global warming, we all know this is happening. Also much like global warming, there are many arguments about *why* it is happening. I tend to think some of these arguments are ludicrous. Here's why.

WOMEN TEND TO GO INTO LESS LUCRATIVE FIELDS

It is true that women tend to go into less lucrative fields. Jobs in fields like education and domestic work pay far less than opportunities available in science, technology, engineering, and math (STEM). It is also true that we have a cultural tendency to encourage our daughters towards these lower-paying fields and fail to nurture and praise talents that could one day be used in the higher-paying fields. We tend to do the opposite with our sons.

I am not going to sit here and tell you that you shouldn't encourage your daughter towards STEM professions. If that is where their interests and talents lie, or if it's not but your child simply wants to get money out of their career rather than passion, I personally think it's a good idea. I would say the same for our sons.

However, I also think we need to look at this issue on a deeper level. *Why* do fields like education and domestic work pay less? I'd argue that it's less about the importance of the work and more about inherited cultural norms we don't even think to question.

Teachers, for example, are in high demand in many parts of the United States. The profession requires a quality education and skills beyond content knowledge. You have to actually be able to apply the concepts you learned about in school to your work and interactions with human beings. Those human beings will grow up to be taxpayers and hopefully innovators who push our societies to what we hope will be higher planes of moral and material comfort. We all want our children to have a better life than we did, and a huge part of making that happen is getting a good education from skilled teachers.

Yet this profession notoriously pays low wages. Over the past year, there have been multiple teacher strikes across the country, often in some of the lowest-paid regions.

Compare this job to one in a field like transportation, storage, and distribution management. Making up 83.5 percent of its workforce,[31] men dominate this well-paying field, working on logistics and transportation of goods for businesses, including in the gas and oil industry. While this is undoubtedly an important job—especially if you're transporting something like oil or gas—I personally do not think it's inherently more important than educating the youth of tomorrow, yet the median salary is over $30,000 more.[32]

Another example is domestic work. In America, more than 90 percent of workers in this labor-intensive field are female, and immigrant populations are disproportionately represented.[33] Keeping in mind that many workers in this industry have employers who illegally pay under the table—presumably at lower-than-legal wages—and therefore do not have their wages reported to the government, the average weekly wage of domestic workers in private households in the fourth quarter of 2017 was $398.72.[34] Adding insult to injury, female domestic workers are often subjected to physical, sexual, emotional, and/or verbal abuse within the households where they work.[35]

Compare this to a field involving manual labor where men typically work: construction. Here, the average American weekly pay in the fourth quarter of 2017 was $977.99/week. That comes out to about $24.45/hour if you assume a 40-hour work week, and you may also have benefits and protections as an employee, especially if you're in a union. I don't want to paint too rosy of a picture—this field has its problems, too. In particular, opioid addiction tends to be high, but that is another issue for another day.

The average domestic worker gets paid less than half the amount that the average construction worker earns, and neither job is great for your body long-term. One field is dominated by women, and the other by men.

When we look back on our liberation as women, we have to think about the work we used to do for free. Domestic labor and raising children was the work of women—and our society and cultural norms dictated that we did it all for free. Education was one of the first fields where women were able to find some equal footing, but again, the compensation in this field tends to be low. Men, on the other hand, had their value assessed by their ability to bring in an income and provide for their family.

So which is truer: that women gravitate towards fields that pay less, or that we as a society value the fields that women are traditionally encouraged towards at a lower dollar amount?

It's probably a little bit of both. But when we recognize that the field has been devalued because of the gender that's dominated it rather than the actual value of the work, we can take steps towards fixing the system rather than placing the blame squarely on the shoulders of young women as they choose their career paths.

WOMEN DON'T NEGOTIATE

Part of the reason women don't get paid as much is because they don't initiate salary negotiations as often as men—right?

It turns out this widely-held belief is little more than a myth. In a joint study between the University of Wisconsin, the University of Warwick, and Cass Business School, researchers discovered that women do in fact ask for raises just as often as men. We're just 25 percent more likely to get rejected.[36]

Part of this is because social norms tell us that women must act in a certain way. We are simultaneously told to ask for what we want and condemned for being too pushy when we do. Be sure to read the next chapter to learn how to navigate this Catch-22.

WOMEN HAVE BABIES

This is the biggest excuse you'll hear put up for the wage gap. Women have babies, and therefore biologically have to take time off of work. Then, cultural norms encourage her to stay at home while the child is younger, be the parent to call off work when the child gets sent home sick from school, and otherwise be the caretaker first and the professional second.

These norms can stunt women's careers because of what their superiors imagine women's decisions will be rather than because of how women exercise agency over their own careers.

"Having a child meant that I wasn't committed to my company," says Zahariadis, remembering another painful incident in her career, "and the opportunity to apply [for] the position I wanted was taken from me."

It is true women need time off of work to recover from childbirth. But in all my years trying to prove that maternity leave causes the pay gap, I have not come up with logical evidence that the gender pay gap is biology's fault rather than systemic discrimination. If this argument were true, then when we looked at the gender pay gap across the world, those with the longest and most generous government-mandated maternity leaves would have the largest gender pay gaps—wouldn't they?

In the United States, the only federal government policy that protects expectant and new mothers in the workplace is the Family Medical Leave Act (FMLA). It allows for up to 12 unpaid weeks off. Your company cannot fire you or give your job to someone else— unless they offer you a similar position at a comparable salary upon your return.

To qualify for this leave, you must have worked for your company for at least a year, and they must have at least 50 employees. You don't qualify if you're part-time; you can legally lose your job for taking time off to give birth if you work less than 26 hours per week. This disqualifies 44 percent of working women,[37] many of whom are in situations of disadvantage and may not be able to build up savings to cover their basic expenses while they are recovering from childbirth—much less after they lose their jobs.

The World Economic Forum evaluates the gender pay gap across the world, and their 2017 report[38] ranked America 49th—where number one is the smallest pay gap. We're directly below Botswana, Uganda,

Bangladesh, and Peru, and managed to have a slightly smaller gap than Kazakhstan, Jamaica, and Zimbabwe.

Meanwhile, in Canada, mothers get up to 12 weeks off *before* they have their child. The mother or father may take parental leave for up to 18 months. If you condense this leave to one year, you will be paid 55 percent of your normal earnings up to $543/week. If you choose to spread your leave out, you'll receive 33 percent of your pay per week for 61 of those weeks. Even with this policy, it is estimated that outside of Quebec—where maternity and parental leave policies are far more generous—38 percent of Canadian mothers don't benefit from this program. Imagine making $36,000/year. On leave, you'd be pulling in $1,650/month, which might allow you to pay your rent or mortgage, but not much else. The further down you get on the pay scale, the stickier it gets—though at a certain point you may start qualifying for other benefits.[39]

Canada, which gives mothers far more time off than the US along with the added benefit of paying them, has a gender pay gap ranking of 16. That is not to say that there is a negative correlation between maternity leave policies and the gender pay gap.

If that were true, then Rwanda, which provides only 12 weeks of maternity leave—though paid at 100 percent—wouldn't rank number 3 in the world for pay equality, far above Canada. And if that were true, then France—which offers 16–26 weeks of fully paid maternity leave—wouldn't rank below Rwanda at number 11 despite giving new parents more paid time off.

We could go through this for a while—there are 144 countries on the World Economic Forum's list. But the point is that although I am not a mathematician, I have found no positive or negative correlation between maternity leave policies and the gender pay gap. In fact, I've found no correlation at all.

If it's not the time that women are taking off that impacts the gender pay gap, I think we have to take into consideration that we need to overhaul our opinions and then our systems if we want to get rid of the discrimination that started this myth and stunts women's pay.

Don't rush back to work before you're ready or willing to do so if you have enough money to get by while you recover and bond with your child. Encourage your partner to do the same if you live in a location where state laws or company policies make that possible. The amount of time you take to welcome a new child into the world isn't an excuse to pay you less—the numbers just don't add up.

SOLUTIONS

Now that you've gotten my hot take on the pay gap, I want to introduce you to Chatón Turner. She is an employment and health care compliance lawyer in Pittsburgh who is passionate about closing that gap. We'll get more into salary negotiations in the next chapter, but she proposes four potential solutions to the discrimination against women due to their ability to birth babies. The first is all about reframing maternity leave at a higher level.

"There are lots of things employers pay employees to do that don't directly benefit the organization," Turner says. "Maternity leave should be framed as an employee benefit just like conference attendance. Employers pay for conference attendance to help employees become better professionals. Maternity leave is no different, really. It's helping employees address the needs of their families so that they can contribute in better ways to the organization."

Because many well-qualified, professional women leave the workforce every year due to the maternity and parental leave problem, Turner also suggests that employers who want to increase retention start offering flexible scheduling.

"In hospital nursing, it's a 24-hour business. Nurses can work nights, days, or any combination thereof. They can also work three 12-hour shifts and have the rest of the week off. That's an example of flexibility that helps the company directly, too. For corporate jobs, the organization could identify a 12-hour workday where anybody could work any nine-hour time period of their choosing. That would give mothers the ability to pick up their kids or be there to send them off to school."

Turner also points out the importance of paternity and parental leave policies. She notes that when men take advantage of these policies, childcare is no longer a 'women's issue.' This also helps fathers bond and engage in the caregiving process early on, potentially creating a shift in those cultural gender norms.

Finally, she thinks it would be a good idea if the government got involved.

"There could be a national marketing campaign by the federal government that promotes companies and individuals who invest in the well-being of infants and children, as they are really investing in the workforce of the future."

It may feel unlikely that we will see changes like these implemented widely in the near future, as brilliant as they may be. But when we start talking about them—talking about what we need and what a better system would look like—we can start imagining a different future. And that's the first step towards building it.

TAKE ACTION ⑤

- *Challenge traditional ideas and your own thoughts on the gender pay gap. Then, read the next chapter to learn about one of the most effective ways we currently have available to battle it as individuals.*

CHAPTER VIII
The Subtle Art of Negotiation

Because you are, in fact, worth it.

One of the proposed arguments justifying the gender pay gap is that women don't negotiate. As we found out in the last chapter, that just simply isn't true. Women attempt salary negotiation just as often as men, but they are 25 percent more likely to be turned down.[40]

When I look at a lot of the negotiation advice I've seen over the years, a lot of it is coming from the male perspective. The assumption is that because men ask for raises more often, they must be the experts on making negotiations work. It's a logical assumption, but it fails to address gender expectations and how they might be the reason women are less successful when initiating these conversations.

For that reason, I reached out to two master negotiators, both of them female. They don't just negotiate for their own pay; negotiation is literally a part of their job definition as lawyers.

Chatón Turner, the employment lawyer from Pittsburgh, suggests negotiating with your HR department rather than your boss or supervisor.

"You don't have to work with HR every day," she says, "so there's a different energy to it. [Also, know] that men and women perceive women who negotiate salaries differently. Women have to ask 'in the right way' or it's perceived negatively. Women have to smile and be nice. I know that's infuriating, but it's true. And it adds to the stress."

Rebecca Neale, who practices family law in Boston, concurs. In fact, Neale has spent time compiling a series of tips and advice for women specifically through the lens of these cultural views; she encourages women to be confident without being perceived as too aggressive.

SANDWICHING YOUR ASK

Knowing that men and women are regarded differently in the same context is the first step to figuring out how to frame your request for more money.

"With salary negotiation or raise negotiation—you do have to ask carefully," says Neale. "You can't ask the same way a man's going to ask for it. Because whether we like it or not, we are swimming against this tide of social constructs where women [supposedly] don't ask, where we're apologizing for asking for what we're worth because at many levels we're told we're not worth as much when that's simply not the case."

Unfortunately, at the present time we're going to be most successful when we accommodate these sexist constructs. Maybe in the future our culture will change to a point where men are not compelled to be aggressive and women are not penalized for doing the same. But for now, Neale recommends a method called sandwiching.

Essentially, sandwiching means you'll be putting something before and after your request for a raise. Neale recommends that the "before" part include positives such as why you love working for the company or that you're excited about the ways you have been able to contribute to the company in the past year. Then will come your ask, followed by some quantitative data. This could include things like your sales numbers, what others with your experience level earn in your region, or any data you have on how you've improved the company's profile or bottom line.

To review, you'll:

1.   Give a positive framing, such as why you love the job or what you're happy to have contributed.

2.   Ask for a pay bump.

3.   Provide quantitative data to justify that pay bump.

"We do have to be cognizant that we can't just come up and say, 'I'm worth more. You have to pay me more,'" says Neale. "You have to sandwich the ask between behaviors that are more gender stereotypical for women. It's a delicate process, but if you couch it in those kinds of feel-good [i.e., I love working here...] and authoritative terms [with quantitative data], you're more likely to be a success."

FAIRNESS, APOLOGIES, AND COOPERATION

Neale was recently negotiating for a writing position. While she does take on some work creating online content, it takes a lot for her to do so as her billable hours as a lawyer are so highly paid. If writing doesn't pay as much, it's hard to justify spending time at it. She explained this to her potential client, quoted them her rate, and then almost made a misstep.

"I was about to say, 'I'm sorry.' And that's what I don't want anybody to be saying. I don't want anyone to be apologizing for asking what you're worth. Thankfully, I was on the phone so they couldn't see how I was shaking my fist—I can't believe I was about to apologize! When I'm face-to-face, I try to just smile after I've quoted my rate so I can't say anything after that."

As women, we're culturally conditioned to think we're not worth as much—that we have to apologize for asking for what we're worth, because surely that's an inconvenience for someone else. But what happens when we do that is we end up undercutting ourselves and ending negotiations prematurely.

"It makes it look like you don't deserve what you're asking for," Neale explains. "If the other party doesn't think you deserve it— doesn't think you're worth as much as the market rate—then they're less likely to give it to you. They're more likely to apologize back and say, 'I'm sorry. We just can't do that.'"

Knowing that market rate is important. You can find it by doing some research on Glassdoor, the Department of Labor's website or even by looking up other, similar job postings in your area. Neale says that by basing your requested raise or salary on such quantitative data, you're keeping things objective and dodging another thing that restrains women during these negotiations: fairness.

Fairness is decidedly not objective. Everyone's version of "fair" is going to be different, and if we try to be fair to the person sitting across the table from us, we run the real risk of devaluing what is "fair" to ourselves. By basing our requests on quantitative data, we remain objective and hold that person across the table to the same standard.

We're also culturally trained as women to be more cooperative—to avoid conflict. While it's not a fun fact, it is a true one. It makes us more likely to accept the first offer thrown our way when we're entering salary negotiations rather than asking for more.

"Suppress that knee jerk reaction to say yes and instead take some time to think about it—and then counteroffer," encourages Neale. "They have already decided to hire you. They decided to throw out this compensation package, and your job is to see if they can do a little bit better. So, depending on the kind of rapport you have with the company, you can gauge what kind of counteroffer to make."

Some phrases Neale uses include:

- *I was hoping for something a bit higher. Can you do a little better than this?*

- *Is there any room to negotiate?*

- *People in this area with my expertise make $XYZ. I was hoping for a little bit more—is there any way you could get to $XYZ?*

How much you should counteroffer is a subject for debate. Some will tell you to come into negotiations with a number in mind—and then double it. The idea behind this rule is that as a woman, you're likely already shooting lower than your actual value and that this method will give you room to negotiate down to a level where you're actually comfortable with the salary.

Neale, however, has different advice.

"You do want to say a reasonable number," she advises. "You don't want to shoot for the moon—unless the number they gave you is such a lowball that you'd never leave your current position for it. In that case, you could say, 'This is what I'm making here, and if you can't match that I can't leave.'"

GETTING HIRED VS ANNUAL REVIEWS

Prior to becoming a lawyer, Neale was working full-time as a community health educator. The nonprofit she was working for hit some hard times and gave everyone a 4 percent pay cut to help make ends meet.

It was disappointing, but Neale didn't realize how disappointing until she made friends with a new hire. They got to talking about compensation, and Neale found out her new friend had not been given an offer with the 4 percent cut; she was new to the company but was making more money than people who had been there for years. Neale approached her boss about the situation, aiming to get her pre-cut salary back.

"It was unsuccessful, but I learned a lesson," she recounts. "And that lesson is that unfortunately, organizations value new talent more than current talent."

Because it's so much easier to get paid more when a company is courting you—when they're trying to convince you that their organization is the right match for you and your talents—it's important to negotiate before you get the job. If you wait for annual reviews, you're going to have a whole lot less success. That doesn't mean you shouldn't try for pay raises after you already have a job. It just means you should put in your most ardent effort in the beginning.

"Your entering salary serves as an anchor," says Turner, noting that any pay increase you receive thereafter will be based on that initial salary. 3 percent of $50,000 is less than 3 percent of $75,000. "So get as much as you can when you walk in the door."

BATNA

What do you do if your counteroffer isn't accepted? What if your potential or current employer won't budge, even though you politely asked for what you're worth with data to back up your request?

This potential outcome scares a lot of people into avoiding negotiation entirely, but that would be a mistake.

"The thing about a salary negotiation is that they've already offered you the job," says Neale. "The only issue is the compensation. It's extremely unlikely that they're going to say, 'Nah, because you asked for more, we don't want to hire you.' Your worst-case outcome with counteroffering is that they'll say no and you [will] have to accept or reject the offer they gave you."

This, says Neale, is why you need to establish BATNA before you even walk into negotiations. BATNA stands for Best Alternative to a Negotiated Agreement, and it will help you figure out what to do should your employer turn you down.

BATNA is going to be different for everyone. Maybe you really need the job and are willing to accept even if they don't meet your counteroffer. (Though that doesn't mean you shouldn't try. Always counteroffer.) Maybe you're willing to take a pay cut in order to work for this company as the culture and flexibility fits better with your lifestyle.

Perhaps you could even get the company to give you more flexibility than they initially offer. If the company isn't willing to budge on salary, Turner encourages women to remember that benefits can be a huge part of the negotiation process, too.

"Be mindful of everything you want that has value other than money—technology, days off, and other benefits. Sometimes, you can get a bigger signing bonus than salary increase. There's more creativity in negotiating than most people think."

Or maybe you're not willing to leave your current job for a marginal increase in salary at a company with low employee-retention rates and they're not willing to give you anything beyond their initial offer to convince you to come on board. In this situation, you may be okay with walking away.

Whatever you decide, you need to establish your BATNA beforehand. Otherwise, you risk sitting in a conference room immediately after your offer has been rejected without any idea what to say next. Avoid this by making up your mind before you walk into that meeting. Don't let your fear of that awkwardness stop you. Don't convince yourself that they won't be interested in you if you ask for what you're worth. As Neale said, they've already decided to hire you. They want you at their company. You're just hammering out the final details.

You are worth being paid the same rate as men in your position. Your biology doesn't affect that. It's the social norms with which we've been raised that make us think the burden of childbearing makes our work less valuable. Don't fall for that constructed fallacy. Go get yours. The sooner you do, the more money you'll make over the course of your career.

TAKE ACTION 💲

- *Research the going rate for someone of your profession and experience level in your locality.*

- *Prepare any data you may have about how you've added to the company's bottom line or reputation.*

- *Practice sandwiching your ask using Neale's 3-step method.*

- *Practice your counteroffer strategy.*

- *Remove the words "I'm sorry" from your negotiation lexicon.*

- *Establish your BATNA before you walk into the room.*

- *Go rock that salary negotiation.*

CHAPTER IX

Doing My Own Thing

Women are rocking small business in America.

If you're sick and tired of having to prove your worth to an employer, there is another option: start your own business.

You'll be in good company if you decide to take this route. While the small business sector as a whole has only grown by 9 percent since 2007, women-owned small businesses have boomed at a rate of 45 percent over the same time period. What's more, women aren't just breaking out on their own. They're killing it once they go solo. Women-owned businesses have seen a 37 percent increase in revenue since 2007—that's ten percentage points higher than the economy at large.[41]

I want you to enjoy that good news for a minute. Bask in it.

Because unfortunately, there's an asterisk coming up.

WHY WOMEN ARE STARTING SMALL BUSINESSES

We should be really glad women are seeing such high success rates when they branch off on their own. It proves that we can and do succeed in business—an area historically dominated by men. Not only do we succeed, but we build and succeed at higher rates than men. While it's about equality rather than competition, it is nice to see so many ladies proving gender stereotypes flat-out wrong.

However, the reason women are starting their own ventures is not so bright and cheery. It's important to note that the fastest growing group of entrepreneurs is black women. Since 1997, this demographic has grown by 322 percent —an incredible feat which has brought much success and has even more powerfully proved oppression is based in fallacy rather than the reality of an individual's capability. But experts attest that a large reason for this growth is in fact that same oppression. Women of color face a far greater wage gap and more discrimination in the workplace than white women, and they are also affected more heavily by the lack of family-friendly policies at most workplaces in America. It's no wonder so many are breaking out on their own, and it's encouraging and inspiring to see so many reaching levels of success where they can independently support themselves and their families.[42]

Those in the LGBTQIA+ community also face major discrimination in the workplace. In the next chapter, we'll hear from Nicole Lynn Perry, a transgender woman of color, and hear about her experiences as she hunted for a job after transition. She points out that while heteronormativity definitely plays a role in the discrimination she faces, it's cisnormativity that she faces first. Virtually every time she meets a new person or applies for a new job, she is all but forced to come out as transgender, though the fact that she's a lesbian is something paperwork and gender presentation don't necessarily force her to expose.

Nonetheless, up to 43 percent of LGBTQIA+ employees say they've been discriminated against in the workplace because of heteronormativity and their sexual preferences—even when they haven't yet come out.[43] State laws compound this problem as there are only limited protections for this demographic in vast regions of our country. It's not just LGBTQIA+ people who should be concerned about this; states who are trying to attract businesses should take note, too. Over the course of 11 years, (2004 to 2015) more than one million jobs created by LGBTQIA+ entrepreneurs left states with discriminatory laws. Almost 80 percent of them headed to the states of California, New York, and Illinois, where there are far more protections. However, these entrepreneurs often cited additional reasons for their move: being closer to talent, investors, customers, and suppliers along with wanting more economical locations for their businesses were all reasons that contributed to their moves.[44] It may be that states who know how to attract businesses and talent also know that inclusive workplaces and laws supporting those inclusive workplaces are an important draw, along with corporate tax advantages.

Of all the self-employed and small-business-owning women I interviewed for this book, all but one said discrimination in the workplace played a role in their decision to leave their nine-to-five careers. While I knew this would likely be the outcome, it was still heartbreaking to hear. These are quite obviously bright, talented women who bring a lot to the table, and workplace culture is making them feel like they're not wanted. The story has a happy ending: these women have created meaningful ventures with their immense talent, doing well for themselves while doing good for others. But the reasoning behind their departures is enough to make you infuriated with the system.

Ashley Hill, the previously mentioned scholarship search strategist from the Atlanta area, lives in one of the top states for growth of African-American women-owned businesses. In her past life, she was a research analyst in the field of chemical manufacturing. She told me that discrimination definitely played a large role in her wanting to start her own business, coupled with her passion for helping people get a college education.

"It wasn't direct discrimination," says Hill, who was the only minority female in her office. "It was things like purposefully leaving me out of meetings or having me play a part in the project without giving me any guidelines. My first job was for a major company. I would go to upper level management asking for resources and assistance and be told, 'No, you'll figure it out.' It was how men would talk to me and how I was berated in front of other employees. It prompted me to move sooner than I had planned to."

We should definitely be celebrating people like Hill: those who build their own success when the world tries so hard to deny them such achievements. But to admire bootstrapping without addressing the reasons it's necessary is to do a great disservice to women—especially women who face oppression at multiple intersections.

HOW TO BE SUCCESSFUL WHEN YOU BREAK OUT ON YOUR OWN

Women being pushed out of traditional workplaces is messed up. But let's not forget that silver lining: once women break out on their own, they're rocking it. In case you want to give this strategy a shot yourself, I asked some of the self-employed or entrepreneurial women I interviewed about what has worked for them. This is by no means an exhaustive list of success tips; you will want to dig deeper before making the major decision to leave your nine-to-five job. But these are a sampling of lessons learned from real-life female go-getters who have blazed the path before you.

BE FINANCIALLY PREPARED

While women are rocking it compared to the market at large, it is important to remember that only about 50 percent of new businesses make it to year five, and only about 33 percent make it to the ten-year mark.[45] I have total faith that you can do this, but it's important to be practical about your finances, too, as being financially prepared can sometimes be the difference between success and destitution.

Choncé Rhea, the freelance writer from Chicago, kept this in mind as she started out her own venture.

"I landed a pretty good job after college, but I never really felt content or fulfilled," she says. "I became tired of working for someone else and making their dreams come true, and I've always felt like an entrepreneur at heart."

To prepare for her departure from her traditional day job, she paid off as much debt as possible. She also kept her own independent business as a side hustle until she was confident it could reliably provide for herself and her family.

Hélène Massicotte—a Winnipeg native who gains her income streams from efforts in personal training, writing, speaking, and consulting—kept her job in corporate Canada until she and her husband had built up enough savings to be financially independent. She did run her personal training business on the side while still working in her corporate position, but it was the couple's joint savings that gave her the confidence to do what she loved without going into the office to work for someone else every day.

Not everyone will be able to build financial independence prior to starting their own venture, but having a more-than-healthy emergency fund and proving your business model before you let go of the reliability of that cubicle job that pays your bills every month is good sense.

HAVE CONFIDENCE

The confidence Rhea and Massicotte built before breaking out on their own is key to running your own business. If you don't believe you're worth your fees, if you don't believe your product fills a gap in the market, if you don't believe your expertise is valuable, you're going to have a hard time attracting clients or customers.

Hill learned this lesson not by failing, but by succeeding. She noticed a multibillion dollar company's Twitter account and thought she had something to offer them. She wasn't really sure how it would go; she was a company of one reaching out to a mega business. But rather than shutting down the idea or succumbing to the thought that they wouldn't even bother to reply, she mustered up her confidence and courage and sent them a direct message on the social media platform.

"You really have to be a leader," she encourages. "I was doubting myself. I had just come out of a male-dominated industry in corporate America. I didn't know how it would go, but it led to a contract. I was so ecstatic."

Go big. You might just be surprised at how much you can achieve when you put yourself and your business out there.

RUN A LEAN OPERATION

I should note here that across the industries I've worked in my adult life, the vast majority of the time I've operated as an independent contractor. I'm no stranger to this solopreneur game. One piece of advice I've noted over the years is investing in yourself.

It's sometimes good advice. Austerity policies—where you invest nothing into your business—rarely spur growth. But you have to be careful with it, especially if you're running a solo operation without investor backing. Just because you can write something off on your taxes doesn't mean you're not spending money. And not everything you spend money on will directly lead to growth in your business.

Massicotte is a strong advocate of running a lean operation. When she started the personal training aspect of her business, she had aspirations for a brick-and-mortar location. It made logical sense to take on a salaried employee. She wanted to pay her fairly, but she was quickly realizing that doing so was putting her business in the red. Her corporate salary helped compensate and keep things afloat, but eventually she had to get rid of the position and abandoned the idea of renting out a separate location for operations.

"There's a ton of power in operating on a shoestring budget," says Massicotte, "focusing more on your skills and abilities than the flash. I think that running a nimble business with minimal financial obligations is important. You can also work with people on contract—not just as an entrepreneur with a storefront. That's not to say that as the business grows you might not have somebody come on permanently, though."

Be cognizant of your budget. Invest money where you can fiscally afford to do so, making sure your investment will lead to growth. But don't feel like you have to attend all the conferences, take all the courses, join all the paid networking groups, open a storefront, or hire an employee just to be considered legit.

FIGURE OUT WHICH EFFORTS LEAD TO THE HIGHEST PROFITS

Hill also recognizes that you have to focus on those efforts which lead to the highest profits. For her business, she has found that spending money on marketing has led directly to increased sales, so she does focus a strong portion of her time and efforts in this arena.

I would love to tell you how to find out which areas will bring your business the most growth. Will it be marketing, like Hill? Will it be product distribution channels? Will it be that certification test that gives your name professional credibility?

The fact of the matter is, I'm not qualified to answer that question in any meaningful way. I have no idea what kind of business you're starting, and I'm assuming that many stratified sectors will be represented across the readers of this book.

What I can tell you, though, is that there is free help available to help you figure this out. There are so many organizations out there that offer free mentoring to female entrepreneurs and small business owners. Seek them out. Good places to start looking for these services are at local colleges (even if you're not currently a student), your sorority network, local small business associations, and small business incubators in your region. These last two may or may not be exclusively female organizations.

I highly encourage you to dig deep to find those programs. However, there are regions where they will be hard to find. If you've searched and searched and are still coming up with nothing, don't be afraid to reach out to those in your field who are already successful. If they're local, offer to take them out to lunch and use the time to pick their brain. If they're far away, start up a conversation via email. You may have to send inquiries to more than one person, but by and large, you'd be surprised how many business people are flattered and willing to help someone who is up and coming. Draw on that confidence and make a meaningful connection.

NETWORK

Every woman I talked to stressed the importance of networking. Getting to know others in your field and finding the ones who support you can be key to both growing your business and keeping yourself in the game when you're feeling burnt out. The growing of your business component is somewhat self-explanatory, so let's dig into how important experiential support from your network will be as you start your own venture.

Rebecca Neale owns her own family law practice in Boston. Being self-employed offers her the flexibility she needs to manage her family life and interact with clients in the best way she sees fit rather than following the direction of superiors. She recounts the feelings of self-defeat she experienced when leaving the role of employee behind.

In most parts of Canada, women make up the majority of law school graduates and the majority of lawyers within the first five years after graduation. In the US, nearly half of law school graduates are female. This has been true for the past 20 years. Yet, in both countries women are represented at the partner level at well below 30 percent. In certain cases that number dips below 10 percent, and the numbers are unsurprisingly the worst for women of color. Women are entering the same field as men—particularly white men—but they're being forced out of current law firms at astonishing rates.[46]

"I don't think the law firm model works for women in general," says Neale. "Of course, there are women who thrive in that model, but they are the exceptions rather than the rule. I think it's important to frame it as, 'What is forcing women out of law firms?' rather than, 'Why are women leaving law firms?' Because we earned a three-year graduate degree and took a really tough exam—we worked our asses off to become lawyers. Large law firms don't have the flexibility women need. They are built on this model where you need a sponsor in big firms to reach down and say, 'I believe in you—here, go to court, work with the client directly.' If you're not playing office politics correctly—you're not aggressive enough or you're too aggressive—[then] as a woman it's a really difficult line to walk to be deemed a good lawyer."

But the realization that discrimination and the current law firm model were responsible for so many women's departures from large firms was not immediately apparent to Neale when she started her own practice. Only by meeting with her local chapter of the Women's Bar Association did Neale realize that her decision to branch out on her own was not unique.

"I remember sitting around the table with five other women—three of whom are 10 to 20 years older than me and two who were the same age—and all of us had the same story," says Neale. "The age gap didn't matter. Nobody believed in them or gave them that opportunity.

"It was also empowering because you realized, 'Oh, it's not about me.' All that self-doubt I had about my abilities? It's not different from what other women are feeling. I think a lot of women silo themselves thinking, 'This is my unique circumstance. I'm not good enough for this job. If I don't focus on it 100 percent and have a family instead, I won't succeed,' even when they want a family.

When we get together, we realize it's not just us, and there's power in that."

If women are feeling like this in the field of law—where educational history and income levels are quite high compared to the general populace—we can rest assured that women in those industries where there is not as much privilege face incredible barriers, some of which may sometimes feel insurmountable. But networking with other women in your field can help you feel less alone and encourage you to keep your foot in the game when you're feeling like a failure—which you're not.

"Stay with it," Hill encourages. "There will be moments when you want to give up and you'll shed a couple of tears. It's all a part of the journey. It makes us stronger. When we feel that strength, it's our responsibility to encourage other women that they can make it."

TAKE CARE OF YOURSELF

Finally, remember to take care of yourself—not just your business. While hustling to achieve your dream is admirable, you're going to crash and burn if you're not nurturing your own needs.

There's an analogy of our goals being like mountains; if we climb one and reach the summit, we can either take joy in our accomplishments, or we can look out to the next peak and never feel truly satisfied because there's still "more." If we take the latter mindset, we're not going to be our best selves—either as human beings or as business owners.

There's actually data to back this up. Eighty-four percent of managers believe that if workers take time off, when they come back, they are more productive. They think more creatively and are more capable of knocking out any problems that come their way in the course of their work.[47] Even taking short breaks is beneficial— you don't have to wait for a big vacation to recharge.[48] Treat yourself the way Google treats their employees and give your brain time to recover throughout the day—whether that's with a coffee run with a friend or playing a game like you're ten years old.

Rhea fights mental overload by slowing down and focusing on contentment and gratitude. She gives herself a minute, then she comes back ready to tackle the next task.

Hill does something similar.

"I deliberately schedule breaks in my day," she says. "I'm training myself not to feel guilty about it. Another thing I started to do is extending work trips. I recently spoke at an education conference and invited my family down to hang out for two or three days after the conference. Intentional scheduling helped me turn a work trip into a working vacation with the people I love."

YOU'VE GOT THIS

If workplace discrimination has you down and you want to combat it by starting your own thing, know that being a woman is to your advantage. Women have been killing it in business— particularly the small business sector—over the past couple of decades. Remember that you're not alone, even though the journey may at times feel lonely. Reach out to others who have been there, seeking out their business advice and their emotional support. Be ready to offer it to others as well. Take care of yourself and have confidence that in this sector in particular, your gender identity isn't the same obstacle as it would be in traditional W-2 employee positions. I can't guarantee that your business will be one of the 33 percent that make it to ten years, but I can tell you that there are other women out there who had the same doubts who are now making life work on their own terms.

TAKE ACTION $

- *Build an extraordinarily large emergency fund.*

- *Test your idea as a side hustle before leaving other employment to do it full-time.*

- *Make sure you have confidence in your product or services. If you don't, you'll have a hard time attracting customers, clients, and investors.*

- *Build a budget for your business and stick to it. While you shouldn't be afraid to invest in yourself, you also shouldn't fall for the trap that any money you spend on your business is a good investment.*

- *Identify the areas of spending which will produce the most yield for your business. You can do this by seeking out a mentor at a local university, small business association, or small business incubator.*

- *Network both to promote your business and to find individuals in similar situations who will be able to provide you with empathetic support along your journey.*

- *Purposefully schedule in time to take care of yourself and your personal relationships. Running a successful business is great, but if you don't take care of yourself, you will burn out.*

CHAPTER X
Headed to the Coasts

Cisnormativity and heteronormativity affect LGBTQ+ women's finances.

The year was 2008. Nicole Lynn Perry, who also goes by Nicki, was signing up as a data network specialist in the Marine Corps. A year later, she went on to marry her wife.

During her time of service, one thing became abundantly clear: she couldn't go on living her life pretending to be someone she wasn't. She wasn't the gender she was assigned at birth. She was and is a transgender woman, and when she separated from the military in 2012 at the expiration of her initial contract, transgender individuals were still not allowed to live authentic lives and continue to serve.

On June 30, 2016, that all changed. Ashton B. Carter, the Obama administration's Secretary of Defense, announced that transgender people could serve openly. Upon that announcement, most transgender members of the military found acceptance from their brothers and sisters in arms. Even prior to Carter's announcement, about one in five transgender people were serving or had served in the military—making the US Armed Forces the largest employer of transgender people in the nation.[49]

The 2016 announcement came too late for Perry. In 2013, she was going through a rough time personally. She knew it was worth it to be out and to live an authentic life, but she was struggling to keep her marriage together, navigate the waters of her identity as a "baby trans," and stay financially afloat, all while going to school on the Post-9/11 GI Bill.

The year 2014 wasn't much better. Perry's marriage did not survive the year, and money struggles were still an issue. She was unable to concentrate on school with everything going on in her personal life and found herself without a place to live, as her home during the marriage had been owned by her ex-wife's family. Perry wasn't yet out to her father, and her mother was herself struggling financially.

Eventually, she was able to connect with a childhood friend's mother who welcomed Perry into her home, respected her pronouns, and even extended a welcome to one of Perry's friends who also found herself without a home.

During this time Perry tried to find a job as herself, but it was a complicated process. While she was out, her name had not yet changed on her paperwork. Perry notes that when the name on the application leads potential employers to think you'll present as a different gender than the one they see in front of them, there can be biases that come into play.

"I do think there's discrimination against trans people when they go in for an interview, though it may not be visible," says Perry. "Maybe you put in an application online first. The next thing is a phone interview. All of your documents are changed to your chosen name and chosen gender. When you talk to them on the phone, they may think, 'Hold on—I thought your name was Nicole Lynn Perry, but you sound male.'"

According to the 2016 National Transgender Discrimination Survey, 47 percent of survey respondents said they had been denied a job, been fired, or lost a promotion because of discrimination related to their gender identity. This type of discrimination leads to an unemployment rate which is double that of the general population. Extreme poverty is four times more likely to be a part of your lived experience if you are transgender compared to the general population.[50]

Seventy-one percent of respondents said they hid their gender identity or gender transition in order to avoid this discrimination, and that's exactly what Perry did. After getting turned down for positions for which she had applied as her true self, she applied for a position as a dishwasher with the gender and name she was assigned at birth.

"I didn't try to work as myself," Perry says. "I needed money, so I worked there for a while."

After about a month, she was able to find a job with the hospital system. Around this time, she talked with her father—but still didn't come out to him. He gave her an SUV to help out, which is Perry's ideal vehicle. "I like having an SUV," she explains, "because if worst comes to worst, I at least have something to sleep in."

With disproportionate rates of extreme poverty, being prepared to sleep in your car isn't an abnormal game plan. Transgender populations experience homelessness at double the rate of the general population, which makes a vehicle with ample room to lay your head down and shelter you from the elements a valuable asset.

While Perry was appreciative both of her friend's mother taking her in and of the respect she paid to Perry's gender identity and pronouns, there were issues outside of cisnormative discrimination that made the home an unsafe place to stay in spring of 2015. Perry turned to her own mother, who said she could stay with her—as long as she paid half the utilities and rent.

With this more than fair offer on the table, Perry made the move. Her mother lived in a one-bedroom apartment, so Perry went out and bought an air mattress to set up in the living room. During the day, she'd set it up against the unused fireplace to make room for her mother's guests. It was still obvious where she slept, but at least there was room for her mother to entertain.

It was a short-term arrangement, but it worked while it lasted. Perry's work was on her mother's way to work, so they'd carpool. Eventually the SUV died, and repairing it would have cost more than it was worth, so she sold it to the mechanic. This is also the time period when Perry was able to start hormones.

It was crowded in her mother's house, though, so she sought out a new place as soon as she could—six months later. Her first apartment application was denied because of a bad credit score, but the second complex where she applied was more lenient. She would have to pay some extra fees, but she could get a place all her own.

It took the complex a bit longer than expected to complete necessary repairs on Perry's unit, but she was finally able to move in mid-January of 2016. Since she could no longer carpool with her mother, Perry started having to ride the bus to work—and everywhere else. She only needed to make one transfer to commute to work, but to get to her church—which was her second home—she had to take two-and-a-half buses. The time was worth the sacrifice for her, though. She had started attending shortly after her divorce, while she was still introducing herself to the world.

"They were completely supportive of me—my identity, my name," recounts Perry. "When I became a member, I hadn't changed everything legally. Only a few people knew my birth name [for tithing purposes], and they kept it secret. People knew my story, and I was still accepted as Nicole Lynn Perry—female—without an issue."

A supportive community can make a big difference, as it did for Perry. The fact that though she had yet to change her birth name legally, she was still respected as Nicole Lynn Perry made it worth taking two-and-a-half-buses. But changing her name was no small task. In order to change it legally, she had to appear before a judge, which was a gamble in her home state of Texas.

Texas has no hard and fast rules about transgender people changing their names. Everything relies on the whim of the judge. Perry identifies these counties as generally having supportive judges:

- *Dallas*
- *Travis*
- *Bear*

She says many have luck in Harris County as well—though far from all.

"When you go into smaller counties, some have had good luck," says Perry, "but many judges do the name change, not the gender marker change. Texas specifically has name and gender on the court order. In some states, like Florida, you can change your name but not your gender marker."

HOW DO NAME AND GENDER MARKER LAWS AFFECT YOUR MONEY?

You may be wondering why legal names and gender markers on official documents are such a big deal. What bearing could they possibly have on your financial life?

As it turns out, there are tons of real-life implications. "The simple fact that our ID doesn't have our chosen name on it creates problems," says Perry.

Imagine going to purchase alcohol and being carded. If you don't look like the name on your ID, a cashier may deny you purchase. Even items that aren't restricted by age can be difficult to purchase if the cashier thinks your appearance doesn't correspond with the name on your credit or debit card.

Getting that debit card can be difficult in the first place. Banks follow strict "Know Your Customer" (KYC) rules, requiring you to verify your identity seven ways to Sunday. If the person reviewing your application thinks things don't line up, you'll have problems opening an account. Or if your state won't let you change your name, you'll be forced to do all of your financial transactions under your dead name—the name you were assigned at birth. This outs you each and every time you make a financial transaction—whether you're comfortable with it or not.

"It's not the greatest work-around, but the way I did it when I couldn't open up a checking account was a prepaid debit card," says Perry, offering a temporary though undesirable solution. "It's not the greatest way because there may be a fee to keep your money there. There may be a fee whenever you reload."

You may also still run into the ID problem, as Perry once did.

"If you use debit or credit, they will ask to see your ID, and there's not always a name on that prepaid debit card. It said, 'Valued Card Holder,' on one I used last year. Some cashiers will let it slide, but others will say, 'Nope, sorry,' and deny you the purchase."

After succeeding in finding an apartment, Perry at last had her very own place. She also had a friend who needed a roof over her head, and because she has a big heart, Perry welcomed her friend into her home. Even though her friend didn't make much effort to find employment and started inviting her new boyfriend and his friends over, Perry couldn't stomach putting her out.

As time went on, the boyfriend and his friends were over more often. Perry—who is polyamorous—met a new love at a support group and started spending less time at home and more time with her new girlfriend and her girlfriend's wife. Her old roommate moved out but had lost the spare key.

Perry's girlfriend tried to convince her it didn't make sense to keep paying rent at a place where she never spent any time, and when the apartment complex called her with complaints of people coming and going at all hours, she took action. She went back to check on the apartment only to find out that she had been robbed. Her PS3, TV, and pizza maker were gone. So was the air mattress that used to sit against the fireplace in her mother's living room.

Perry didn't feel like she could call the police. She viewed the entire thing as her own fault. She felt she should have drawn harder lines and been aware of what was happening in her own home. The apartment had been damaged, but she and the apartment complex worked out a way to break her lease, though her inability to pay for the repairs did end up further damaging her credit score.

At this point, she moved in with her girlfriend and her girlfriend's wife, though she had to sleep on the couch. They made plans to move to Colorado together. Things felt so solid that Perry gave notice at the hospital.

After her last day at work, things started to fall apart in the relationship. Some months later, she once again had to find somewhere to stay—and now she had no employment. The hospital had already filled her position, and the job hunt she had planned for Colorado was never to be.

Another friend was kind enough to open up her home to Perry. She and her wife offered Perry their spare bedroom free of charge. Without a vehicle, Perry's job hunt was slow. Taking the bus to get to interviews was time-consuming, but she continued trying. There was tension in the house as the months dragged on, though no one wanted to say anything about it. They mostly kept away from each other to avoid any potential confrontation. Because Perry felt so guilty about not contributing financially, she rarely ate. She recounts a time when a friend gave her a can of beans and that was all she ate for the day and instances where she would try to eat so little that no one would notice she had been in the cabinet—even though her hosts never denied her food.

In March of 2017, there was an uproar about the bathroom bill legislation in Texas. Perry, who was still without a job, figured that she might as well use her time to support the cause. She became deeply involved in activism. Other activists would give her rides to Austin to fight the discriminatory law; when she was home, she still spent the bulk of her time seeking employment—and trying to round up bus fare so that she could do so.

After months of no success, she created an exit strategy.

"Between the bathroom bill, Trump making his tweets [specifically regarding transgender individuals serving in the military], and me being a black trans woman, it wasn't safe for me there anymore," says Perry. Her home state of Texas had the highest rate of murder of transgender women in 2017. "But I had no savings."

She had several friends in Washington state and began to consider moving there. As she tried to get a game plan together, some of them moved away, but she finally decided to move in with a love interest. Unfortunately, the relationship turned sour before moving day, and she found herself frantically searching for a new place to live. Reluctantly, she started a GoFundMe to help her get out. She was able to find a friend who had an extra bed in Washington, but because it had taken her so long, a lot of the GoFundMe money had to go towards her bills in Texas. So she wasn't flush with cash, but she did have a little left over get to Tacoma at the tail end of 2017.

Upon her arrival, she immediately started interviewing. She didn't meet with much luck until a couple months in, when she got a part-time gig as a sorter at Amazon. She continued looking for additional work with assistance from Minority Veterans of America and another veterans' organization. When we last spoke, they were helping her do things like get her LinkedIn profile up-to-date as it hadn't been edited since prior to her transition. Since we last talked, she has found stable housing in Seattle.

"I want to have my own place," Perry told me while she was living in Tacoma. "I don't want to be an imposition on someone else. Even renting a room is fine. At least I'd be financially contributing, and it's better than couch surfing."

HEADED TO THE COASTS

Perry's move to a more accepting locale isn't unique. In the US, many LGBTQ+ individuals choose to move to coastal cities. It tends to be safer there, and there also tends to be less job discrimination.

According to Jennifer Chan, a lawyer in Toronto, there is a similar trend in Canada, though individuals don't always head to the coasts; they head to bigger cities in general. She also notes that regardless of sexual orientation or gender identity, younger people tend to flock to the cities, where there are more jobs.

Living in a place where you're safe is hands down the most important thing when you're trying to live an authentic life. However, living in a major metropolis almost always comes with higher costs of living.

"The main thing I think about a lot being in a gay relationship is that a lot of financial advice today talks about geographic arbitrage," says Taylor Milam, a resident of Southern California. "'Move here! Move there!' they say. 'Go live in this little-developed country,' or, 'Go live in a tiny town in the middle of nowhere.' I think that that advice is a little bit insensitive—or not realistic for people depending on their identity or their sexuality or their gender presentation. To use that as blanket advice isn't applicable to everyone. Especially not to LGBT people."

Milam has lived in an area with a high cost of living for a while now. She acknowledges that there are accepting people everywhere, but is also cognizant of general cultural differences in cisnormative and heteronormative discrimination levels in less urban areas when compared to bigger cities. In that spirit, she has some advice for those looking to cut costs.

"If you want to live somewhere that's more expensive, whether it's because you're LGBT or for another reason, you are going to have to prepare yourself for the cost of rent because that's going to really be the big difference. That number is pretty much set. In the bigger cities in Southern California, for example, you're not going to be able to live anywhere safe or comfortable for under an average of $1,500 per month for a one-bedroom."

Milam notes that rent is the only thing that's set in stone; you have a lot of control over other costs. She encourages people to exercise their financial agency by deciding what the most important big money expenses are, and conversely, what are the things that don't matter as much to you personally. Here are some areas she suggests examining first:

- *Lowering your grocery costs*
- *Cooking at home more often*
- *Packing your lunch for work*
- *Lower your transportation costs*
- *Reducing your commute*

You can also prioritize your wants. Milam uses shopping and travel as an example. If shopping is important to you, you might not have the budget to jet around often. If travel is more of a priority, you'll have to dramatically cut back your shopping habit.

She encourages those considering a move to an area with a higher cost of living to start practicing these skills now. Use coupons for groceries. Cut down how often you eat at restaurants. Stay away from the mall so those plane tickets will be within your reach. That way, when you do make the move, you'll be more prepared for the frugal lifestyle you'll need to adopt in order to get by.

Of course, landing a high-paying job will definitely help, too. Perry has some career suggestions for those looking to make a geographic jump to a safer—but more expensive—area.

"I worked as a help desk specialist, but really anything in IT can be taken anywhere," she says. "Even if someone [only] has a small business, they probably want to get set up online or at least have a web presence. Health care is another good field."

Perry's personal experience and instincts match the data. If we look at information from the Bureau of Labor Statistics for Seattle,[51] San Diego,[52] and New York City,[53] health care positions—especially those requiring a doctorate—and computer science jobs top the list as far as gross annual compensation. Also in the mix are:

- *Airline pilots, copilots and flight engineers (Seattle)*
- *CEOs (San Diego, NYC & Seattle)*
- *Architectural and engineering managers (San Diego)*
- *Natural science managers in research and development (San Diego)*
- *Sales Managers (NYC)*

SO YOU'RE TELLING ME TO BE SUPER RICH AND SKIP LATTES?

Ugh. I know. I think that kind of advice is really annoying and tone deaf, too. Too often it skips over the real and varied obstacles presented by cisnormativity, heteronormativity, and other flavors of oppression.

But those obstacles aren't going anywhere anytime soon. That's a statement I make with a heavy heart—and I hope the passage of time will quickly prove me wrong.

Until things change, though, seeking out professional training in one of these fields is likely to improve your odds of securing high-income employment. It doesn't make it a guarantee, but it does make it more likely. If you're dead broke and can't imagine returning to school, check out Chapter 4 to find out how you can go for free.

And skipping the lattes won't improve the lot of the impoverished. But low-income households are headed by some of the best money managers I know. You know you shouldn't dine out three times a week, and you know you should use grocery coupons. Maybe you are already cutting costs in these ways. But sometimes, the stress of not having enough money to go around encourages your brain to make decisions for convenience's sake. Don't beat yourself up about it. It's natural and happens to a ton of people living through what you've been through.

But also know that there is hope. Taylor is making it work in SoCal as she pursues a career in education. Jennifer has established a meaningful career for herself in the legal field in Toronto. And Nicki continues to strive towards her dreams in Seattle. I know she's going to make it, and I have faith that clinging to hope will provide better—though not always easy—financial outcomes for you, too.

TAKE ACTION 💲

- *If you're considering moving to a different city for reasons of safety or employment discrimination, do some research on the Bureau of Labor Statistics' website to see which jobs are both in demand and pay well. Work to get the education and training you need to pursue those fields.*

- *Practice living on a tighter budget today. Stash away any money this saves to help you pay for moving expenses and/or to build up an emergency fund.*

- *If you're a veteran seeking employment, check out organizations like Minority Veterans of America and other LGBTQIA-friendly organizations that can help you get that job.*

- *Connect with the local LGBTQIA community to figure out where you should file for name and gender marker changes. The experiences of others will help you find the path of least resistance. That doesn't mean no resistance—just less.*

- *If cisnormative and/or heteronormative discrimination doesn't affect you, remember the real-life lessons you learned through Perry's story. Educate yourself on ways to become an ally and effect change.*

PART THREE

SAVE MORE

CHAPTER XI
Buy This, Not That

I'll buy whatever I damn well please—as long as it fits into my budget.

I am not going to tell you where you should and shouldn't spend your money. We get enough input on that, especially as women. There is pressure to keep up appearances—to dress a certain way, to raise our children with certain material goods or experiences, and to cover bills instead of splitting them, because that must mean we are better friends. At the same time, we are often shamed for indulging ourselves, even if the purchases we make fit into our budget.

How dare you take pleasure in a spa day!

It must be nice to take all those trips.

You pay how much in rent just to put your kid in a good school district?!

To be honest, I don't care what you spend your money on. I'm not going to judge you based on the frugal or extravagant lifestyle choices you make. But because I care about your financial future, I do want to show you how to make these decisions wisely and stay within your budget.

THE McCLANAHANS ARE COVERT JONESES

Thirteen years ago, Aja McClanahan and her husband were sitting on a mountain of consumer and student loan debt. They didn't really appreciate how precarious their financial situation was. When they found out they were expecting, they made the joint decision that McClanahan would be a stay-at-home mom. She was doing some small things outside the home like homeschooling the neighbor's kids, but she wasn't making any meaningful money for it.

A few months after their daughter was born, they got a terrifying letter in the mail. It notified them that her husband's wages were going to be garnished to the tune of $700/month. His student loan debt was catching up with them. They were already on a limited income and weren't sure what they were going to do now that paying back the loan was going to be a forced decision outside of their control. Would McClanahan have to reenter the workforce? Would they have to put their daughter in daycare despite it not being the ideal decision for their family?

It was during this dark time that McClanahan heard a radio program that changed her life. It was a Dave Ramsey special focusing on how to pay off debt. While I personally don't agree with all of Dave Ramsey's financial philosophies, it is undeniable that he has helped an inordinate number of people dig their way out of debt and build solid financial futures—especially people of Christian faiths.

"I was hooked," says McClanahan. "I needed this in my life. We went through Financial Peace University [a Dave Ramsey course] and became debt free!"

To get out of debt, McClanahan put her educational background in Spanish to use and started tutoring. She listed household items on Craigslist and eBay. Of course, they also trimmed their budget down as much as humanly possible. Part of that involved moving in with her mother in a south-of-Chicago suburb, which eliminated rent or mortgage payments.

During that time, her family inherited a home in Inglewood—which was one of the top three worst neighborhoods in the inner-city portion of Chicago at the time and was full of abject poverty and extremely high crime rates.

"'Thanks, but no thanks,' we thought," recollects McClanahan. "We wanted a house without a mortgage, but we didn't want to move into a war zone. But financially, it made sense for our family. I'm a praying woman, and the answer we received was to make the better financial move."

When they announced their decision to their family, they were met with shock and concern.

"My parents were like, 'What is going on with you? It's dangerous there!' People thought we were nuts—insane. We came from two really nice suburbs northwest of Chicago. From there, we had moved into my mom's in a south suburb—it was still a very nice community."

But the McClanahans moved forward with their decision despite the negative input. Living without a mortgage allowed them to not only completely eliminate their debt, it also allowed them to build the lifestyle they truly wanted. Today, McClanahan homeschools her children. They are able to take their education on the road through a practice called roadschooling. In 2016, they took trips to the Dominican Republic and San Diego as they studied ecosystems, marine life, and rainforests. They spent six weeks in California was as they visited the San Diego Zoo, Sea World, and more. In 2018, since their oldest child is studying different types of government, the plan is to head to Cuba for hands-on education opportunities.

"We live in the ghetto with no [mortgage] notes," says McClanahan, "so we can do all that debt free."

Their lifestyle also affords her children the chance to explore one of their interests and potential future career paths: acting. Chicago is known as the city second only to New York City for its TV commercial productions and opportunities for young dramatists. McClanahan's children have been featured in several commercials and voiceovers, for which they are earning their own income and learning how to manage it with guidance from their parents. The family has taken investing classes together and has learned more through free online resources on sites like YouTube and Udemy. If you ask her eldest daughter, who at age 12 has already invested in Exchange Traded Funds (a type of mutual fund also known as ETFs), what she wants to be when she grows up, she'll give you two answers: a famous actress and a stock broker.

That being said, McClanahan wasn't sure about the decision at first. She remembers her uncertainty the first time they were purchasing headshots.

"'Lord, is this something I should be doing?'" she remembers asking. "But because of my availability as a homeschooling mom, I'm able to support them in that. Because of where we live, we can drive to downtown Chicago in 20 minutes with traffic. The fact that they invest their money in brokerage accounts, choosing some funds or stocks? That's been a cool consequence."

Aside from setting up their own family financially, the McClanahans' move has allowed them to build a meaningful life in their Inglewood community. The neighborhood has seen improvements over the eight years they've lived there. The 'war zone' neighborhood is on the rise. According to McClanahan, crime rates have dropped dramatically, and unemployment rates are lower than they were when the family first moved in.

The family has dedicated a good portion of their time to helping make those improvements happen. She's plugged into the local church, and despite homeschooling her own children, she's also involved with the local high school. Because Chicago is such an expensive city to live in, her family is not the only one that's chosen to move to a neighborhood that would otherwise be commonly overlooked. The McClanahans have banded together with many such families from different neighborhoods around the city to hold local government accountable for their efforts in these neighborhoods, which has directly led to investments in development.

McClanahan still gets flack over the neighborhood she lives in. When she goes to write a check, the recipient will see the area she's from and examine the payment with extra scrutiny. Before she had her address updated on her license, people would see where she had lived before and where she now lives and ask her, "What's wrong with you?"

But moving to the neighborhood has paid off tenfold. McClanahan can stay home with her kids and homeschool them. The family lives a debt free lifestyle while still being able to travel extensively, thereby expanding their children's education. Her children are able to pursue their interests in acting, earn their own money, and make financial decisions about what other families would consider to be advanced concepts like the stock market while still under her care. Just recently, McClanahan and her husband bought another property as an investment, paying for it with 100 percent cash, and their next big goal is saving enough money for her husband to retire early. On top of all that, they've built a meaningful life as advocates of their community and have had enough freedom of time and money to see those efforts bear fruit.

You could say the McClanahans are secret Joneses. You might not know it to look at their address and their home, which they have fixed up extensively—but that "crazy" decision they made eight years ago has allowed them a lifestyle with freedoms that most of us would envy.

JACKIE LIKES CARS. GET OVER IT.

That's not to say that you *have* to make the same types of decisions as the McClanahans. They arrived at their decision after much consideration of the circumstances of their own individual family, along with their faith in their God's guidance. Knowing that stories like theirs are possible can open our eyes to new potential opportunities for freedom, but if you have the money to fund fancier lifestyle choices, you need not feel guilty in pursuing them.

Jackie Cummings Koski is a divorced single mother, an award-winning author, and a respected professional in Dayton, Ohio. Over the years, she has educated herself on investing and has saved up enough money to be comfortable after living her childhood in poverty. She has always been conscious of her money, but in 2014 she broke her ankle and had to take a break from work while she was on short-term disability. During that time, she fell down a rabbit hole while browsing some financial content online and learned some ways that she could make her money even better.

"I was a saver, but for the first time I created a net worth spreadsheet," she recalls. "I was well over $300,000. Now that I [had] found my numbers, I was more focused than ever. I have no debt. I have a mortgage that's very reasonable. I didn't spend my career as an entrepreneur, but I could retire early on my income."

Koski's income fluctuates but generally falls in the median range for American households. After her divorce, she educated herself on investing and made extremely wise money decisions that set her up for where she is today. That doesn't mean she's willing to give up a career she loves, though.

"I need a bigger cushion to make that decision than most people. I'm not retiring yet."

Koski arrived at her current financial decision through wise money management techniques and investing. She maxes out her retirement accounts. She has everything set up to be as tax-advantaged as possible. But it might surprise you to know that frugality is not one of her priorities.

"Frugality isn't the only way you can do it," she says. "Sure, I'm money-smart, but I go out to eat and I'm not a coupon clipper. My house is what most frugal people would say is 'too much house.' But

I've been in it for a long time and almost own the thing outright. I have two Lexus vehicles in the garage, which I got for 50 percent off of what they cost brand new, and I plan on keeping them forever. We are the only ones who can manage our own unique set of circumstances. I'm already at financial independence. You can do it many different ways."

Oftentimes as women, we're labelled as shopaholics who spend money frivolously because we love all the shoes. In reality, the odds of being a shopaholic are eerily similar regardless of gender. Women are 6.0 percent likely to be shopaholics compared to men's 5.5 percent likelihood.[54] Just because a woman spends money doesn't mean she's doing something self-destructive.

In fact, budgeting expert and special needs mother Joyce Zahariadis reminds us that spending money on ourselves can be good for our well-being. While women are commonly pressured to take care of others before themselves—especially if they're mothers—busting that gender norm can lead to healthier lives for ourselves and our families.

"We live in a world that somehow makes mom responsible for only focusing on kids and family," says Zahariadis. "We assume that because we are moms we have to take care of others before we take care of ourselves. Instead of feeling guilty, think of it this way: You are taking care of you in order to take care of them. This is something I personally had to do myself. You should of course budget for these expenses or make time for just you. If you want to take the time to play your favorite video game, do it! There is no shame in doing something you personally enjoy that your budget will allow."

BUILDING YOUR BUDGET

Making decisions like those of McClanahan, Koski, and Zahariadis starts with creating a budget. You need to know how much money you bring in. You need to know how much money you're spending on things you don't really need or value versus how much you have to spend every month on fixed expenses like rent, food, and utility bills. And you need to know what your life aspirations and financial goals are.

Let's start with the fun stuff first. What is your next financial goal? Do you want to fully fund your retirement account this year? Heck, maybe you just want to open a retirement account. Maybe you want to plan a great vacation for your family, build an emergency fund, purchase a house, or pay off your student loans.

Whatever your financial goals are, think about them now. Prioritize them. They will help you as you establish a monthly budget.

GOLDEN RULE OF BUDGETING

My entire adult life, I've followed what I call the Golden Rule of Budgeting. It's a simple concept that's engrained in my financial habits, so I was surprised when a short article I wrote about it received attention in several major publications across the continent. Apparently it's something most people haven't thought of before, so I want to be sure to share it with you.

Here it is:

Budget liberally. Spend conservatively.

I told you it was simple. The purpose is to plan to spend more than you think you will, giving you a buffer so you don't find yourself broke at the end of the month. If you think you're going to spend $300 on groceries, maybe budget in $400. If you're planning on spending $100 on entertainment this month, up it to $150 so that you won't be kicking yourself the morning after you bought a couple extra drinks while out with your friends.

Then, when you go about your business during the month, be mindful about your spending. Try to spend less than you have budgeted. Coupons may be the way you achieve your success. You might trim back your clothing budget by going consignment instead of retail. Or, you might just practice some self-restraint and not buy things that you don't actually need.

This golden rule can be applied to any type of budgeting method, and it helps you achieve two things. It allows you to see up front if you have enough money *before* the month starts. If you don't, you now have a little time to volunteer to cover extra shifts at work or pick up a side hustle to make your cash flow situation work. While it is extremely stressful to budget and realize you don't have enough money to make it through the end of the month, it's a whole lot less stressful than getting to the last grocery shopping trip of the month and realizing you don't have enough money to feed yourself.

At the end of the month, if you've worked hard and found ways to source the money you need to fund your liberal budget, your conservative spending should put you in a place where you have money left over. It might be a little or it might be a lot; either way, it's a win. Although ideally your budget will include incremental savings for your financial goals, like a certain amount set aside for your emergency and/or travel fund, you'll now have a little bit extra to throw at those goals, which will get you there faster. By stressing at the beginning of the month rather than the end, you'll actually find motivation to keep practicing good money habits as you'll know there's a reward for doing so at the end of every month.

ENVELOPE BUDGET

All right. Now let's get into the types of budgets to which you can apply this rule. Keep in mind that none of them are universally perfect; you're going to have to choose the one that works best for you. You may even find that after playing around with them for a while, you create your own unique blend that best fits your own unique lifestyle.

First up is the envelope budget. This type of budget is commonly used by those trying to establish newfound financial discipline.

You're going to start the process out the same way you will with writing any budget: write out a list of all of your planned expenses for the month. Remember to make your estimates liberal.

Then, get an envelope for each line item. On payday, withdraw all the cash you'll need to meet these expenses. (Some expenses— like retirement savings or transfers to your savings account—may be best done online on payday rather than via actual, physical envelopes.) Divvy that cash up into each appropriate envelope, and let the conservative spending begin.

Here's the key concept behind the envelope budgeting method: You have a finite amount of cash in each envelope. After it's gone, it's gone. Physically holding the money and seeing how much you have left should reinforce better financial habits. Ideally, you won't borrow money from any of the other envelopes, but if you do, it's a conscious decision that you'll be physically making. Then, the following month, remember how disappointed you felt in yourself when you had to make that decision, and adjust your budget accordingly.

Some argue that the best way to use the envelope method is by using cash, as the physical reminder is what really makes it effective. However, everyone functions differently, and you can find apps and online services which allow you to build a digital envelope budget.

ZERO-SUM BUDGETING

The idea behind zero-sum budgeting is that you're giving every dollar a job. You have a solid idea of how much money you'll be bringing in this month, and you consciously allocate each one before it hits your bank account. This includes setting aside money for savings, retirement, and other financial goals. After you've budgeted in every last required expense and goal, you should have $0 left over. This doesn't mean you're broke. It just means you've consciously allocated every last dollar you will earn.

Zero-sum budgeting is my personal favorite method, and I still use the golden rule with it; I estimate my costs as higher than they are likely to be and put anything extra at the end of the month towards my currently-most-important money goal. But it can be really hard to use this method if you're a freelancer, own your own business, or otherwise have a variable income.

If you find yourself in this circumstance, the best way to use this or any other method is going to be to get a month ahead. That means that at the end of June, when you're budgeting for July, you already have the money you'll need to make it through July on hand. Then during July, all the money you earn will go towards meeting August's budget.

Getting a month ahead may seem like a daunting task, but if you have a variable income, it's one that's going to make your life a whole lot less chaotic. Hustle hard, save harder, and do everything in your power to get to a place where it's possible. It might take you months. It might take you a year or more. But once you get to a place where you have a full month's worth of expenses saved up ahead of time, all that effort will have been worth it.

PERCENTAGE BUDGETING

Percentage budgeting is sometimes known as the 50/30/20 method. The idea is that you spend 50 percent of your earnings on necessities, like housing, food, utilities, etc. 30 percent will go towards things you want, like a night out with friends or that super cute thing you saw the last time you dared to venture into Target—which is always full of all the super cute things. The final 20 percent will go towards your emergency fund, your retirement fund, or any other type of savings.

I'm going to be blunt: This percentage-based budgeting is efficient for a very small demographic. At (more than) one point, I was very low-income, and my rent alone was more than 50 percent of my monthly budget. Savings and extraneous spending weren't even on the table because I was so busy trying to get those basic needs met.

If you're pulling in a larger-than-typical income, percentage budgeting might not be the best bet either. If your monthly pay is $10,000, that doesn't mean you need to spend $5,000/month on your mortgage, groceries, and utilities (unless you want to and you have all your other financial bases covered; no judgement.) In fact, you might want to put more towards your savings and investments, where it can grow and potentially let you out of the rat race earlier if that's one of your priorities.

You know your finances, learning style, and money management strengths and weaknesses better than anyone else. Get started by picking the method you think will work best for you, applying the golden rule to whichever strategy you choose to use. If it's not working for you, tweak it or use another method. The important thing is getting started. We all hit road bumps along the way, but with a budget, you'll be better prepared to handle them as you pursue your own meaningfully wealthy life.

TAKE ACTION ⑤

- *Release yourself from any preconceived notions about what it is or isn't okay to purchase or how to spend or save your money.*

- *Establish a budget. You may want to use the envelope, zero-sum, percentage, or other methods.*

- *Apply the Golden Rule of Budgeting to whatever method you select.*

CHAPTER XII
Why Don't We Insure Against Divorce?
Separate your finances and build your own skill set.

Whether you're hearing them or saying them, they're four of the most painful words in the English language:

> *"I want a divorce."*

When you end a marriage, the future you had planned together dies. It's something you grieve—even if it was you that initiated the split.

Divorce is hard emotionally and financially. Emotionally, I want to let you know as someone who has been there that it does get better. The day will dawn again—you just have to go through the thick of night to get there.

Financially, it can be much more difficult to recover, which is why I like to encourage women to take preventative measures with their finances. You're probably thinking, *"She wants me to sign a prenup?"* or, *"But my marriage is going to last forever!"*

You don't have to go as far as a prenuptial agreement, but unfortunately, you do have to recognize there's a solid chance your marriage won't last forever. Only 52 percent of American women will see their first marriage make it until their 20th wedding anniversary. In other words, 48 percent will experience divorce, separation, or—in the rarest cases—become widows within the first 20 years of their first marriage. Researchers at the CDC say that these statistics have remained consistent since the 1980s.[55]

If you're Canadian, you have slightly better odds. You have about a 40 percent chance of seeing your first marriage end in divorce before your 20th wedding anniversary.[56]

As sad as it may be, the odds are extremely high that you'll get divorced. Yet culturally, we do very little to protect ourselves from the stress and economic risks of this dramatic life event.

To put this into perspective, let's look at some things we *do* protect ourselves against:

- *The most expensive homeowner's insurance claims are caused by fire or lightning, according to the Insurance Information Institute.[57] The odds that you'll experience a fire bad enough to file a claim during the course of your lifetime is 25 percent.[58] Yet we insure against this risk by purchasing homeowners insurance.*

- *If you're an American woman, your odds of dying between ages 15 and 60 are 7.4 percent. If you're a Canadian woman, those odds are 4.7 percent.[59] Yet how many of us—especially the mothers among us—purchase life insurance?*

- *More than 7 percent of Canadians over the age of 15 have a disability,[60] and 25 percent of America's 20-year-olds will have a disability before they retire.[61] Yet we buy disability insurance.*

Okay, that last one is a bit of a misleading. Not many people I know have disability insurance, but it's a good idea to look into it, as disability before retirement is more likely to happen than death before retirement.

But you get the point. All of these things are less likely to happen than divorce, yet we insure against them. The solution is not to stop buying insurance, but rather to insure ourselves in our marriages even if we've wed Prince or Princess Charming.

INSURE YOURSELF WITH SEPARATE FINANCES

Most of us go into marriage anticipating a happily ever after. We don't walk down the aisle expecting to ever get divorced, so we don't take necessary steps to protect ourselves should we become one of the 48 percent of American women or 40 percent of Canadian women who don't make it to that 20th anniversary.

I have good news, though: there is a way to self-insure against tragedy.

Cultural norms dictate that when you get married—or sometimes even when you enter a serious relationship—you make your finances joint. For a long time, this was actually empowering for women, as it gave them access to money they wouldn't have otherwise had since they weren't traditionally permitted in or encouraged to enter the workplace.

But our world has changed. I am a strong believer that the most empowering way for modern women to manage their finances in marriage is by keeping at least a portion of their savings separate.

IT COULD HAPPEN TO YOU

Here's a story about Jack and Diane. A young couple, they walked down the aisle batting their googly eyes at each other. They were so in love, and they just knew they would never fight. Ever. About anything. One of their first financial moves together was opening a joint bank account and closing down their individual accounts. Both of their names were on everything; they shared their bed, so they shared their money.

The years wear on. They age as their youth slowly drifts into the past. They bicker about little things like who did the dishes last, and big things like the question of to whose hometown they should permanently relocate.

Eventually, Jack starts sharing his bed with someone else. Diane is heartbroken and enraged. Both believing the worst of each other, they each race to the closest ATM to withdraw the cash from their liquid assets, like checking and savings accounts. Because both of their names are on the accounts, there is nothing legally wrong with either partner taking all the money. Jack wins the race, and he runs off with all the savings.

Although all assets should be split equally according to the laws of their state of residence, without access to cash, Diane can't afford a good lawyer. She ends up giving up a lot of ground in court, and she walks away with only a portion of the wealth she's spent years building with Jack.

And yet, life must go on.

Sounds horrific, right? Unfortunately, it's a situation I've seen more than one woman go through over the course of my life. Cheating isn't always the catalyst for the split, but it's alarming how often lack of access to capital ends up putting one partner at a massive disadvantage in court.

There are a few different ways to do this, and the path that's right for you will be completely dependent on your individual needs and relationship.

The first approach is to not put your partner's name on anything. Keep all of your financial accounts separate. In many states, assets that you build together or that experience growth during the course of your marriage will be subject to splitsies regardless, but you'll each maintain whatever cash footing you have, so you'll have access to money for a good lawyer should your divorce end up in court.

Note that keeping your finances separate does not mean you don't have joint goals. You'll have to work together to figure out who is paying for bills A, B, and C and who is paying for expenses X, Y, and Z. You will need to dream together about home ownership, vacations, retirement, or whatever your life goals may be. You'll need to work out how each partner will contribute according to their income, and if one partner doesn't work, you'll need to figure out how to allocate a fair or even generous amount of cash towards their own independent savings account.

You can also set up partially separate finances. In this setup, you do maintain joint accounts for things like bills, rent, mortgage payments, and kids' activities. You may also have a joint savings account for your family emergency fund, and you may add your partners' name to loans and assets you acquire throughout the course of your marriage.

However, at bare minimum, you each need to keep your own individual savings account. You allocate money from your big joint pot towards these accounts every month, and you do so equally. Each partner can spend or save that money as they wish, though saving it is highly encouraged.

What you've just read isn't a popular opinion—even within the personal finance community. I've seen the whole "share your bed, share your money" phrase thrown out countless times as if it's some type of doctrine with blind disregard for the hard numbers.

The biggest argument against separate finances that I hear is, "Well, I guess you just don't trust your partner, then. I'm starting my marriage out on a basis of trust."

Trust is a major part of any successful relationship, and we should all start our marriages from that mental space. However, I think you can both trust your partner today in the here and now and also maintain enough respect for yourself to acknowledge the hard reality that you may not be with the same person in 20 years.

You can trust your partner until you can't anymore, but you can start respecting yourself today.

I also want to emphasize that separate finances are not something you should be doing behind closed doors. All of this should be something both partners fully understand, and both should be fully on board with these arrangements. When both partners acknowledge the risk and agree to some form of fully or partially separate finances, what I see isn't a lack of trust, but a whole lot of love and respect.

Essentially, when you separate a portion or more of your finances from the other person's, you're saying:

> *"I know there's an almost 50 percent chance I may hurt you someday. I don't plan on ever joining that number, but I love you and respect you enough to encourage you to protect yourself. I'm not going to take offense."*

SOLUTIONS FOR HOMEMAKERS

As we discussed back in Chapter 1, being a homemaker is an extremely valid life choice. It does, however, raise the issue of how to handle some potentially trickier situations when it comes to managing separate finances.

In these cases, you're probably going to want to implement partially separate finances rather than wholly separate finances. Have the other partner's pay deposited into the joint account, and then allocate an equal amount of savings to each of your separate accounts from there. I'd almost argue that the homemaker should get a larger portion for savings as they're in a more precarious position with a gap in their work history, but that's something for you to work out as a couple.

As a homemaker, it's also important to make a point of keeping up your career skills in case you ever have to rely on your own income rather than your spouse's. Here are some ways you can do that:

 Pursue CEUs. *Continuing education units, or CEUs, are offered in many fields as a way of keeping up on the most current strategies used to execute your job. They're typically offered as a way of maintaining certification. When you attend any given training that offers CEUs, you'll likely be offered an opportunity to pay a higher premium for a certificate testifying that you attended and earned the educational credit.*

• CEUs themselves won't land you a job, but they will show potential employers that you're up-to-date with current best practices. Keeping up is a good idea anyway; should you have to (or decide to) return to work, you don't want to have to play catch-up on decades' worth of changes in an instant.

 Pursue Part-Time Work. *Maybe you can't work full-time, but you have a little time each week which you could conceivably dedicate to keeping your foot in the door with a part-time job. If you can't find anything locally that fits your schedule, be sure to look online as many companies now hire remote workers. As long as your work can be done via*

internet, you may not have to leave your home to clock in. If you're having trouble finding work as a part-time W-2 employee, consider freelancing. Maintaining even just one or two clients at a time keeps your work history current. With the rise of the gig economy, you're more likely to find jobs as a freelancer than you would have been in years past.

 Pursue Volunteer Work. *Look around your community for opportunities to keep your skills sharp. If you're a bookkeeper, the local little league organization may need a treasurer. Are you a grant writer? See if there are any local nonprofits you support that could benefit from your services once or twice annually.*

• Administrators might find ways to maintain their record of leadership skills by serving as president of any number of community organizations, and CPAs can volunteer with their local United Way once per year to help low-income families file their taxes. If you pursue this route at any point, remember that you'll need to bluntly and concisely relate how these volunteer experiences demonstrate skills relevant to your career path as well as your ability to achieve in your future resume.

 Maintain Relationships Within a Professional Group. *Knowledge and skill are huge contributors to finding a new job. But equally important is networking. Find a local professional group—preferably one specific to your field—and attend meetings regularly. Build relationships, and show an interest in what the organization is doing. Should you ever need or want to return to the workforce, these relationships will do more to help you find a new position than just skill on its own.*

• Doing these things may help alleviate some of the judgement you'll be met with when you present a resume with a gap, but they will not do the same thing for your career as actively staying in the workforce. Many families need someone to stay home with the kids. If that's you, fabulous. If it's your partner, that's fantastic. Just make sure you're aware of the potential long-term consequences to your financial autonomy when you make this major life decision.

If you're years and years into your marriage and have been managing things jointly to this point, bringing up the idea of separate finances may cause more tension than it's worth. Ideally, we'd all be able to talk about money openly and honestly without taking things personally, but there are a lot of emotions around both personal finance and in marriage.

You know your marriage better than anyone else: if bringing up this topic would make the other person overly concerned with your intentions or cause unnecessary strife, it may be better to let things be.

However, if you're just starting a relationship or your marriage is new, it's likely that this is a conversation worth having as you establish how you're going to manage your marital finances for (hopefully) the rest of your lives.

INSURE YOURSELF WITH MARKETABLE SKILLS

Let's say you *don't* have separate finances; or that even if you do, you have a massive gap in your work history after choosing to stay home with the kids.

This is a rough situation to find yourself in, since eventually, what savings you do have are going to run out. You need a way to sustain yourself. You need a way to bring in money long-term.

Terry Hekker learned this lesson the hard way. She met her husband when she was quite young. A law school student, he was a smart match, and the two went on to have a wonderful relationship and marriage for a very long time. Hekker decided to be a homemaker, which was more of a cultural default when she was raising her children in the '70s and '80s.

During this time period, women were entering the workplace and a wave of feminism was sweeping the nation. Hekker, feeling the need to validate her own decision to work as a homemaker, wrote a book in defense of housewifery called *Ever Since Adam and Eve.*

The book brought her into the spotlight, as many saw her as the standard bearer for traditional family values. Its 1980 publication even secured her an appearance on Oprah.

Fast forward to her husband's sixtieth year. For the first time, he indulged in alcohol—a glass of wine. That one experience led him down a path of alcoholism, culminating in an affair and divorce papers. With that, the forty-year-old marriage was over.

"I had no way of predicting all through my marriage that I was going to be on my own," says Hekker.

CHEATING WITH MONEY

There are many different types of infidelity. Your spouse may commit sexual infidelity, emotional infidelity—or even financial infidelity.

Financial infidelity is when you lie about money, either directly or through omission. One partner may have debt they don't disclose to the other partner. They may drain the savings account, open accounts in the other's name without their knowledge, or even hide money they earned in a secret account. Here are a few real-world examples of this fiscal type of cheating:

- *Your spouse gets a bonus at work but hides it in a secret savings account. It's fine to have a separate savings account, but in a healthy relationship, it's not okay to hide it from your partner.*

- *Your partner becomes addicted to pornography. Ashamed, they feel like they can't tell you about it, but they continue to spend money on it. Eventually they run out of credit. They use your social security number to open a new credit card and start charging subscriptions to pornography websites to your name without telling you about any of it.*

- *Your spouse has a gambling addiction they've been hiding from you. It started out innocently enough in their minds: $20/week to spend at the casino on the way home from work. From there, it balloons to $50/week, $100/week, $200/week— until your joint savings is completely wiped out.*

- *Your partner gets fired from their job but doesn't tell you. Instead, they start driving to a friend's house during the day when you think they are going in for their work shift. You only find out about a month later when the paychecks stop.*

The solutions to financial infidelity are complex and varied depending on your situation. A spouse who finds out about debt is going to have a very different path to fiscal recovery than someone who has just found out their partner has been hiding their pink slip. When your savings is gone, you need a very different game plan when compared to someone who has had their identity stolen.

You may decide the financial transgression is too big of a lie to overcome in your relationship, or you may decide to try to work things out. Many couples address this violation of trust through couples counseling.

One of the best ways to catch this type of infidelity early is by being an active and engaged part of your family's financial management. Look at bills. Look at credit and debit card statements. Keep tabs on your savings account. Check your credit report every year.
Not only will these steps help you catch any financial infidelity early, but these habits are also essential to mastering your own money.

Hekker was elected mayor of her village around the same time as the divorce. While the job gave her something to focus on besides the devastation imposed by the failed marriage, it only paid $8,000 per year. The experience changed her perspective completely, leading her to write her second tome: *Disregard First Book*.

When I asked Hekker for her advice on this matter, she made the very astute point that while building separate savings is good, having marketable skills you can draw upon is potentially even more important.

"The thing about having your own bank account is that bank account will start to be depleted very quickly," she points out. "You've got to have something that will bring in a steady income."

While Hekker, 85, had a degree herself, she notes that when she was growing up, a young woman's goal was to find a man with "good prospects"—not necessarily to find a career for herself. Even with a degree, Hekker didn't have anything marketable in the way of job skills when divorce came knocking on her door.

As time has gone on, cultural norms have changed. Hekker's eight granddaughters—among whom are a nurse, an MSW degreed social worker, and two teachers—are most certainly honed in on careers that would lead to economic self-sufficiency. She glowed when she talked about their efforts, as all of them are "working to be fiercely independent."

If you don't have a degree and you're low-income, flip back to Chapter 4 to learn how to go to college for free. If you are in the same educational situation but at a higher income level, keep reading through Chapter 15 to learn how to do the same thing.

You cannot rely on your partner's salary to be there in perpetuity. Yes, you may encounter divorce, but you may also encounter any number of other life tragedies, as Hekker pointed out during our conversation.

"If you are marrying Prince Charming, he might not be Prince Reliable," she says. "The other piece is he might be the best guy that ever lived, but he could be hit by a car. He could die. He could develop an illness where he's handicapped and can't [work]. Lots of things can happen. Life has a way of throwing curve balls at you."

If you haven't yet curled up in a ball and set this book down as you sob, I do want to remind you that 52 percent of American marriages and 60 percent of Canadian marriages do make it to that 20th anniversary. Not all marriages fail, and there's a good possibility yours might be one of the successful ones.

But the odds of misfortune are high enough that it only makes logical sense to prepare your finances and your own money-earning capabilities in case the worst should happen.

TAKE ACTION $

- *Think about the pros and cons of separate financial accounts on your own. Weigh the merits and potential problems, and assess your risk tolerance when it comes to a 40 percent (Canadian) to 48 percent (American) chance of divorce within 20 years.*

- *Talk to your partner about having separate financial accounts—particularly a separate savings account. You may want to skip this step if you're years and years into your marriage and you don't think it will be productive. But if your love is relatively new, it's a step that may be worth pursuing.*

- *Think about ways you can build or maintain your own skill set. Will you get a degree? Look for remote freelance work? Join a new professional organization? Pick one course of action to get started. Then, come back to this exercise and commit to a second way to strengthen your future resume.*

CHAPTER XIII
Get Your Middle Finger Ready
Build that emergency fund.

The importance of savings cannot be overstated. Having a cushion can help you whether those funds are to benefit you, your partner, or your entire family. It can help you cover unexpected expenses, turning what would have been a financial disaster into a minor inconvenience. Savings can help you take advantage of opportunities at the drop of a hat. Having savings also fortifies your independence when you need to remove yourself from a toxic relationship—whether that be at work or at home.

Saving is key to living a wealthy life, yet a study showed that 57 percent of Americans couldn't handle even a $500 emergency with their savings alone.[62] Of course, we need to recognize that wage stagnation and income inequality are large culprits at the heart of this matter. It's a heck of a lot harder to save money when you don't have enough to cover your bills every month. I'm not going to sit here and shame you for not doing the impossible.

But we do still have to talk about the basics. Most financial experts recommend that you have at least enough to handle three to six months of expenses saved up in your emergency fund. This helps you cover your bare-bones expenses should you lose your job or become unable to work for a time. It also helps to have that money there when you get an irreparable flat tire or have to take an unexpected trip to the emergency room on an ACA Silver Health Insurance Plan.

Saving up three to six months' worth of expenses is ludicrous when you're not making enough to make ends meet today in the here and now. But that doesn't mean you can't get started with small amounts. Your emergency fund may take you years to build up to the three-to-six-month level if you're living near the poverty line, but if you don't start saving today, you'll have no money stashed away in the same amount of time. Years are going to pass anyway. You might as well have something to show for it—even if that something is small.

SAVING WHEN YOU DON'T HAVE A LOT OF MONEY

When I first had my children, I was living well under the poverty line. When I found out I was expecting the first time, I did something I never had before: I applied for benefits through my state. It was a lot to handle. First, I had to get over the fact that I wasn't independent. I couldn't provide for myself and a child on my own, and that felt humiliating.

But that child needed to eat and deserved prenatal care, so I humbled myself and did it anyway. Then, there was the paperwork process. My county assistance office did everything they could to not process my paperwork. Keeping up with it all felt like a full-time job in and of itself.

And then there was the asset test. At the time, the value of our family's second car (which allowed both of us to have a job) combined with any money in our savings and checking accounts could not exceed $5,000. We had to be very careful not to save too much money, or we risked losing things like SNAP benefits. Luckily, in the past several years most states have eliminated many of their asset tests. There are still some stragglers out there, but by and large the asset test conundrum has been lessened.

Even in the age of rampant asset tests, though, we found ways to build up marginal amounts of savings. I did several side hustles, including volunteering for medical studies. Many of them were psychological and just looked at my or my baby's behavior. There were no substances going into our bodies, and there were no long-term effects. We qualified for these studies by virtue of who we already were. That money sometimes went to paying bills, but sometimes it went towards building that emergency cushion.

We also used a common trick with our coins. Anytime we spent cash and got change back, that change went into a container. At least once a month, I'd roll the change by hand. This allowed me to save on Coinstar fees while keeping an eye out for any rare coins that might be worth more than their face value. Because we utilized a fair amount of cash back then, I would sometimes find myself rolling hundreds of dollars in a single night.

A third trick is to automate your savings. Even just $5/week can build your emergency savings to $260 over the course of a year. It's not three to six months' worth of expenses, but it's still something. According to research by the Urban Institute, having even $250-$749 in savings lowers your chances of being evicted, missing a payment on a bill, or even having to rely on public benefits.[63]

To set these transfers up, hop online or call up your financial institution to automatically transfer $5 from your checking account into your savings account every Monday, Friday, or whatever day of the week works best for you.

To supplement this savings habit, look to nonprofits like Earn (earn. org) which encourage and reward saving—even in small amounts. Earn's SaverLife program gives you cash for initiating your own savings habit. When you save $20/month, SaverLife will give you $10/month for free. Your rewards are distributed after six months, so you'll get a lump sum of $60 after you've saved up $120 total over that same period. It's free money from a national nonprofit whose mission is to help Americans build a sounder financial future.

You may be able to find similar programs in your locality. Sometimes they are known as family savings accounts. Sometimes your welfare office, YWCA, or United Way will know how to connect you with the organizations that offer these rewards. When you've got someone else pitching in on your emergency fund, you're going to be able to build it up that much faster.

LIQUID COURAGE

Not all women sit on the brink of poverty. If you're lucky enough to be bringing in a higher income, it's time to start thinking bigger when it comes to your emergency fund. This money can not only help you avoid financial ruin should you run into the unexpected, but it can also help you to gain more freedom and live life on your own terms according to your own values.

When you build your emergency fund to a point where it's large enough to tell off your boss, an abusive partner, or anyone else on whom women have traditionally found themselves economically dependent, it's commonly redubbed a "F*** Off Fund," as in, "My boss told me I had to start working Sundays or I was going to lose my job, and then how would I afford my pretty little shoes? So I told him to f*** off. Sundays are mine, and I can buy shoes without his measly paychecks."

That would be a pretty badass position to be in, right?

Of course, even if you have a F*** Off Fund, burning bridges isn't always a great idea. And it's not always appropriate to use the f-word when you're explaining your finances to family members or friends. That's why Hélène Massicotte, a Winnipeg-based personal trainer, writer, and speaker, repurposed the term 'liquid courage.'

Massicotte grew up in a home where she felt the effects of family finances being stretched too thin. Her mother had moved to the capital city of Ottawa to serve as a government interpreter while her father continued his work in Winnipeg, which resulted in the family supporting two households instead of one. As a result, the family took on credit card debt, and her father started looking for roommates to live in their Winnipeg home. At this point, Massicotte, who was then a teenager, moved to Ottawa with her mother before the family was reunited in Winnipeg about a year later.

It was in Ottawa she first started feeling the strain. Massicotte never wanted for food and was spoiled on birthdays and holidays, but she noticed the financial struggle her parents were going through, and it scared her.

"I didn't ask for *anything*," Massicotte recalls of her time in Ottawa. "Life was that tight. I was just happy for a two-liter of Diet Pepsi and gummy bears on Saturday as a treat during our grocery shopping, our one and only weekly outing. I even refused my mom's offer of bus tickets to get me to school because I knew she couldn't afford it."

Her parents had side hustles and projects they were always working on to try to right things. When Massicotte's father passed away, she was just 19 years old, and her mother hit further financial bumps in the road after his passing.

"There are a number of months before financial accounts are unfrozen if you don't have power of attorney for your spouse," explains Massicotte. "I saw my mother have to jump through hoops with the bank. She couldn't make mortgage payments. I'm guessing she was living on credit cards."

Massicotte took some time off from university to help run the family businesses before returning to school and entering the corporate world around age 24. While she did have a Retirement Savings Plan (RSP) through her employer, she opened up a separate investment account where she had more control over where her money was going. She continued this practice after switching employers thirteen years later even though she now had a defined benefit plan (also known as a pension). The experiences of her formative years left her wanting to leave nothing to chance. She would be in control of her financial life, and she wouldn't look over the precipice of potential financial ruin again.

She established a rule for herself—the burger-flipping rule. Her new financial goal was to get to a point where she could do whatever she wanted for the rest of her life and be just fine financially—even if that thing was flipping burgers.

FINANCIAL INDEPENDENCE AS AN EQUALIZER TO GENDER INEQUALITY

When we look back through recorded Western history, often we see women treated not as equal citizens, but rather as property to be traded through marriage. Men, on the other hand, have had to establish their worth not through their looks, family connections, and dowries, but rather through their ability to bring in an income. Massicotte points out that we shouldn't ignore the pressure this puts on men, as they have historically mainly been valued for their net worth and ability to provide financial security for women. That is a burden to bear.

But she also points out that among other arguments for self-actualization and freedom, women remain at a greater financial disadvantage. When children are born, we are still culturally expected to be the ones to stay at home, though this is gradually changing. We are paid less for doing the same jobs. Because our value hasn't historically hinged on our individual net worth, a far greater predictor of our assigned value to society has been beauty and physical attractiveness. It's not right, but it's unfortunately true.

Massicotte sees divorce rates as a big problem for these reasons. As people of all genders age, their beauty changes in ways society doesn't always appreciate. Even if a man feels responsible for your financial security today, he may not ten or twenty years down the road. To establish financial security for yourself as a woman is to take a huge leap towards gender equality.

"Being able to stand on your own two feet—even if at the moment you shouldn't or don't think you have to—is critical," says Massicotte. "The need is there. It is real. We need to have savings to have options. We should never have to stay in a relationship or have a relationship severed with nothing to fall back on. We need that savings because marriage is no longer a financial security default due to high divorce rates. That's a big, big change to our social fabric over the past two generations."

Over the years, Massicotte can retrospectively identify some mistakes she made while investing. But the important thing was that she was steadily socking money away and making saving for the goal of financial independence both a priority and a habit.

At age thirty-five, Massicotte returned to school. Her mother had experienced a scary heart event, and as it had been a heart attack that had taken Massicotte's father, she wanted to learn more about the human body and keeping it operational. Her next degree was in kinesiology. Four years earlier, she had hit a major milestone—she had met her burger-flipping goal and now had hit the magic number to establish "liquid courage." She had enough money and assets to live on for twenty-five years, so taking a leave of absence to complete her studies was a nonissue.

After completing her degree and returning to work, Massicotte started a personal training side business out of her home. She worked and continues to work with everyone from teenagers to clients in their seventies, putting her education to use as she helps them live healthy lives. It's something that brings her joy, so when there was a management change she wasn't fond of almost a year after she had returned to corporate Canada, she decided it was time to draw on that "liquid courage." She decided it was time to go. The day she received her year-end bonus was the day she put in her resignation. Her company was shocked, but she was careful to avoid any ill will.

"Over the years, did I encounter some jerks [in corporate Canada]?" Massicotte asks rhetorically. "Sure. But I have to say [that at] the last company where I worked, that was not a big problem. One of the reasons I joined that firm was because it had women on the board of directors and the CFO was a woman. I just knew that's where I wanted to really try to get a job. During my time there, about half the time I had a male boss and about half the time I had a woman as a boss. I really feel the level of professionalism was similar across the board. We are not always in a situation where we can be picky over what our next job is going to be. I was very lucky. If my search had extended six months or more, I might have loosened those requirements. The advice that your emergency fund should cover three to six months? No. It should be years. The higher you go in the pay echelon, the harder it can be to find a job."

With Massicotte's high pay and high savings rate, she was able to establish her 'liquid courage.' It was also a huge help to have a husband who was also a saver. She was able to use their savings to move on from a situation she wasn't crazy about and is now able to use her time to perform meaningful work. She writes for her own site and for a major finance content hub. She also continues her personal training business while at the same time keeping a toe in corporate Canada through speaking gigs and financial coaching.

"Being able to sleep soundly at night is priceless," says Massicotte. "The fact that we don't have debt, to know we don't owe anyone anything [and that] if there is an emergency of pretty much any kind, we're fine—I can't express it enough. Having experienced scarcity both in my family's health and finances, I really do not want to go back there."

We could sit here and dissect each of Massicotte's investment options. She herself readily admits that at points in her life, she spent money on status items to keep up appearances at work. But ultimately, what led to her ability to jump from a work situation she wasn't in love with into a life brimming with fulfilling work was the fact that she was saving a good portion of her income.

The more you save, the more freedom you will have. While money isn't the key to happiness, the ability to pursue fulfilling work is certainly a huge factor in your overall contentedness.

TAKE ACTION $

- *Start setting aside money for your emergency fund, even if it's just $5/week.*

- *Sign up with Earn's SaverLife program and get paid up to $60 for consistently building your savings.*

- *Look for other similar programs in your own state or locality. If you don't know where to get started, ask around at your local YWCA or United Way.*

- *If you earn a high income, save as much of it as you possibly can to build up your own "liquid courage" as Massicotte did.*

CHAPTER XIV
Wait, Am I Part of the Kyriarchy?

We need to educate our daughters—and ourselves—
about investing.

Know what's fun? You can be morally opposed to the kyriarchy and still be a cog in its machine. Before you become "woke," it's totally possible that you're unwittingly participating in sexist cultural norms which are so normalized that you don't even realize what you're doing is wrong.

A great example of this is in the world of investing. We know that while parents don't talk to their kids about investing very often, when they do, they're far more likely to initiate such conversations with their sons than their daughters.[64] It's no wonder that when girls grow up—despite the fact that they'll live longer and therefore will need more money in retirement—they aim lower than their male peers. While men aim to save $400,000 for retirement, women—who are less confident in their investing abilities despite being better at it[65]—set a goal of only $200,000.[66] Neither is enough for retirement, but the fact that women on average set a goal half that of men is telling.

We need to ask ourselves if we are talking to our daughters about investing. If the answer is no, we have to change that. We need to instill in them the confidence they need to build monetary wealth as they prepare for retirement in an age where defined benefit plans (aka pensions) are disappearing. Today, most people are going to have to make investment choices on their own and exert self-discipline to max out their 401(k), IRA, 403(b), RSP, or other tax-advantaged retirement account.

There's a hitch, though: How do you teach your daughter about investing when you don't know much about it yourself? After all, odds are you were once one of those girls who grew up without any education on the stock market. You might even be one of the women setting your retirement goal to half that of your male peers.

We have a moral responsibility to educate ourselves on investing. It's not just about saving for our own future; it's about being a good role model who can pass knowledge on to the next generation.

WHY SHOULD I INVEST IN THE STOCK MARKET?

I'm a millennial who came of age at the peak of the Recession. I was petrified when it came to the stock market. I saw my friends' parents lose big chunks of wealth from their retirement funds and had family members who were directly affected by the housing crisis. I was not interested in gambling my money away, so I figured I'd keep my savings in an FDIC-insured bank account where it was safe and sound. Sure, it wasn't likely to grow as quickly, but it was also far less likely to disappear.

As I entered this field, I learned a lot about the importance of investing and how unfounded my fears were. As you read, I want you to keep in mind that I am a writer who has done heavy research in the area of personal finance over the past seven years, but I am not a certified advisor. Take my words as a springboard for further research, and don't discount the knowledge of those who have successfully pursued those certifications.

First of all, even when the market drops as it did in 2008, it has historically recovered and even gone up in value. If you're investing for the long haul, temporary setbacks aren't a concern, because while some years you'll lose more than the average amount of money in the market, in other years you're likely to gain more than the average.

Another problem with my original way of thinking was the returns. In my post-recession savings account, I was earning almost 1 percent interest. However, the average rate of inflation is 3 percent per year. Inflation was eating my money away more quickly than it was gaining interest. It was the perfect example of one step forward, three steps back.

Investing earns you far more money over the long haul. A conservative estimate on the average interest you'll earn per year is 6 percent, though some people prefer to estimate these returns as 8 percent. Those returns beat the average inflation rate of 3 percent handily.

That being said, there are no guarantees. It is completely possible that the US stock market will crash, burn, and never recover. But if that happens, your paper money isn't likely to hold much value anyway. You'll be too busy fighting zombies and putting your survival skills to use to worry about the NASDAQ.

THE BASICS

There is not enough room in this book to take a deep dive into all the terminology and intricacies of the stock market. But know this: for all those convoluted terms and hacks, the stock market is easier to understand than Wall Street would have you believe. There are three general rules you should know:

1. Don't try to beat the market. The most successful investment portfolios are those which do not engage in frequent trades.

2. The market has historically always gone up over time. If you notice TV pundits shouting that the market is "down," don't freak out. Keep investing as you normally do. When you're saving for retirement, you're playing the long game, and there are going to be some bumps along the way.

3. Start investing as early as you can. Compound interest is your best friend, and it needs time to work its magic. Max out your retirement funds in as many years as you possibly can to take full advantage.

If you can adhere to those principles, odds are you'll be able to meet your retirement goals through investing. (Though again, there are no guarantees.) To adhere to those principles, you will want some knowledge of a number of pretty basic terms. To help explain these, I asked for the helps of Jackie Cummings Koski.

Koski is a sales executive for a global data company based in Dayton, Ohio. When she and her husband divorced, she had $60,000 in her retirement account. At that moment, she vowed to herself that she would learn all she could about investing, and she went on to build her portfolio to its current $180,000. She wanted to set a good example for her daughter and even wrote a book for her called *Money Letters 2 My Daughter,* for which she was awarded a Congressional Commendation for her efforts in financial literacy by the US House of Representatives.

"When I wrote the book, my daughter was 14," says Koski. "I wanted to make sure I could explain concepts to her in ways she would understand."

Today Koski takes that same easy-to-understand language into high schools, colleges, and community centers as she teaches others—particularly African-American women—how they can follow the same path she has. She has also been kind enough to break down some of the basic terms for us today. Here are Koski's explanations of some of the most common terms you'll see thrown around in the world of retirement savings.

- **Time horizon.** *Time horizon is the difference between saving and investing. Saving is when you need money pretty quickly—in one year to four years. You want to keep it safe and not put it at risk, so you put it in a savings account. In* the stock market, you can lose your money if you're investing short-term. But if your time horizon is five years or more, invest the money and watch it grow. Know that it won't grow in a straight line; there will be ups and downs.

- **Asset allocation.** Sometimes when I teach workshops, I'll hear something along the lines of, "I want to buy stock in Google!" I hear the excitement in their voice, and I don't want to temper it. Of course you **can** buy Google, but if it goes down right after you buy, you will not be happy. You can allocate your assets across different investments, maybe get Google, Facebook, and Nike, etc. That way you own a little piece of all of them; if one goes down, you won't be too worried about it.

- **Stocks.** When you own a stock, you're a part owner of the company. If you really like your Michael Kors bag and think a lot of other people would like it, too, you can invest in their stock. If you're willing to spend money on the purse, you can actually own part of the company.

- **Bonds.** When you purchase bonds, you don't own a part of the company. Instead, you're lending them money. Bonds tend to be safer investments that offer lower returns.

- **Mutual funds.** Mutual funds are just baskets of stocks put together by an investment firm or fund manager.

- **Index funds.** Index funds are essentially mutual funds that have a little bit of a lot of stocks. The most common are S&P 500 index funds. The S&P 500 measures the value of the stocks of the 500 US companies with the most capital. When you invest in an index fund, you're buying a little bit of each of those companies with just one investment.

- **REITs.** In real estate investing there are two main ways you can invest. The first is to buy a property. You might rent it out and collect rent every month, purchase a house and flip it, or physically own an asset that is your home. Some people don't like to mess with all that—I know I don't. That's where REITs come in. There are groups of other people doing the physical work of owning and managing apartment *buildings, malls, and other types of properties across all other real estate specialties. You can provide them with funding. You buy an REIT like a stock; I go online and buy from my broker.*

You're also going to want to understand your retirement plan. Maybe you're offered one through your workplace, or maybe you are self-employed and need to set one up for yourself. Here are some of the types of tax-advantaged retirement accounts in the US according to Koski:

- **401(k).** *A 401(k) is sponsored by your company. In most cases, your company will match a certain percentage of your contributions. You are allowed to contribute up to $18,500/ year, or $24,500/year if you're over age 50. The match money that your employer puts in doesn't count towards this IRS limit. Your contributions will go in before taxes, but you'll have to pay taxes when you take the money out in retirement.*

- **SEP IRA.** *You can open a SEP IRA when you own your own business or are an independent contractor. You can save either $55,000/year or 25 percent of your income—whichever is less. SEP IRA contributions are difficult to figure out since you don't know what you'll make until the year is over, making it a good idea to work with an accountant. This money will not be taxed until you take it out for retirement.*

- **Pension.** *If you're 40 or older, a pension may have been available to you. For most people under 40, however, that's not a choice anymore, unless you work for the government— and there are a few other exceptions. Retirement savings used to work differently. You'd be employed by one company, work there for 30 years, and then get a set amount of money every month until the day you died. You didn't have to worry about managing your investments. If you worked with the company for the required number of years, you'd get a monthly check for the rest of your life.*

- **403(b).** *If you work in education or for a nonprofit, your employer may offer a 403(b). It's similar to a 401(k).*

Your employer will give you a list of investment options, and you will have to choose which ones you want. Some 403(b)s come with an annuity component. An annuity is an insurance product that will give you a regular annual payment—sort of like a pension. But with an annuity, there's a certain amount of money you have to pay in first. It's a way to make you ration your money. Annuity contracts are fairly lengthy, and they tend to come with a lot of fees and extra charges.

You can also invest in a **Roth IRA**, which you open as an individual rather than through your employer. The most you can invest is $5,500/year, though those over age 49 can invest up to $6,500/year. The money you put into your Roth IRA will already be taxed, so you won't have to pay any taxes when you take it out of your account in retirement.

If you're a member of the military or a federal employee, you'll be offered a **Thrift Savings Plan** or **TSP**. TSPs operate in much the same way as 401(k)s, except you'll have six investment options unique to these plans. These options tend to be less expensive to purchase than those in 401(k)s unless you have index fund options within your 401(k). Depending on your job description, you may qualify for a 1 percent to 5 percent match from your employer.

CANADIAN RETIREMENT PLANS

As in America, defined benefit plans are on the decline in Canada. There are two accounts you're far more likely to run into: the RRSP and the TFSA.

At first glance, **Registered Retirement Savings Plans** (RRSPs) are similar to the American 401(k). You put money in before taxes and will pay taxes upon withdrawal. You can save up to $26,230/year. While we aren't going to get into the rules of making a withdrawal in this book, that is the one of the largest areas where RRSPs differ from 401(k)s.

Tax-Free Savings Accounts (TFSAs) are more similar to Roth IRAs. You will put money in after you have paid taxes on it, but then you'll be able to withdraw both that money and the interest you earn without having to pay taxes in retirement. The amount you can contribute bounces around every year; this year, it is $5,500. One cool thing about these accounts is that if you are only able to contribute $3,000 this year, you can carry the remaining $2,500 limit to the next year. So if in 2019 the limit is again $5,500, you would be able to contribute up to $8,000 in 2019.

WHAT ELSE CAN BE DONE?

Bear in mind that the definitions we've reviewed in this chapter are not complete and that there are other investment terms and types of retirement accounts out there. Hopefully this 101 primer has cooled down some of your investing anxiety, though, and has inspired you to learn more—and to make sure you're passing on your newfound knowledge to the next generation.

But beyond educating yourself and your children on investing, what else can be done to close the investing gap? Koski thinks you're on the right track simply by virtue of reading this book.

"When I was at a conference one time, we did a little survey with men and women about how they felt they did as far as investing. Men have a little bit more confidence even if women know just as much as men. The women tended to be more reserved and not as braggy—they weren't going around pounding their chests. But they were just as smart and knew just as much. It's about building up confidence. If there are areas you're not good at or don't understand, there are many resources these days. You now have the ability to go and google anything and get all the info you want. Take advantage of the fact that you can go and look it up. The investment world makes it all sound very hard, but it doesn't have to be."

She also thinks that the lack of female representation in the investing world is a big problem. Men tend to cater to male clients, whom they view as having all the wealth and interest in the field. But over the past few generations, women have fought for the ability to build their own wealth, so this paradigm needs to shift. As more women enter the investment realm—which has a similar culture to that of the field of law, as we discussed in the last chapter—more women are likely to be comfortable investing as they see themselves represented. Koski knows this goes beyond gender and can extend into race and/or socioeconomic class.

"I feel like it's part of my responsibility as a woman of color to reach back to my community," says Koski. "I work with any type of organization that works with women of color, underserved communities, or African-American communities as a volunteer. I want to bring them something they probably don't get anywhere else.

"When I'm in these communities, I tell my story of how I grew up in poverty. I'm someone they can see themselves in. I think that [even] before I say a word, that might resonate with them, because we tend to navigate towards people who are something like us or something we aspire to be. If I were the same old white male, I might not connect with them as well. When we grow up and do well for ourselves, we are representing the community. When we become very skilled in certain areas, we have a responsibility to give it back—to share it."

In case you're wondering, the teachings Koski offered to her own daughter were not in vain. Now a young adult, she is stellar with money and has a fierce independent streak. For two years, Koski tried to take her daughter out to lunch while she was interning, but she refused, saying she wanted to pay her own way. She uses Acorns—a FinTech investing app—to invest on her own. While the app isn't her mother's favorite teaching tool, she is grateful that it's opening her daughter up and giving her hands-on experience as the next generation strives to build its own future.

The future is female. And money savvy.

TAKE ACTION ⑤

- *Educate yourself on investing. Start by rereading this chapter, and then continue your learning on your own via your preferred medium: podcasts, writings, or video, etc.*

- *Make sure you're saving as much as you can in your own retirement account—max it out every year if possible.*

- *Because as a culture we tend to talk to our sons about investing more than our daughters, make sure to make a concerted effort to talk to all of your children equally about investing—preferably frequently—regardless of their gender.*

- *Pass your knowledge on.*

CHAPTER XV
Instilling Faith

Saving for your kids' college education.

We all know the cost of college is skyrocketing. And we all know that we should be saving so our children will be able to attend. But that's really hard to do when you're living paycheck-to-paycheck.

Besides the lack of funds, the common advice is to fund your retirement accounts before you fund your child's education. I tend to think this is good advice, as both of these major life events are going to affect your children. Yes, ideally your children will go to college, as it is likely to dramatically increase their income over the course of their lives. But if you retire without enough money, there's a strong chance your children are going to end up supporting you in one way or another, whether that's inviting you to move in with them, paying for your medical care, or taking time off of work to be your personal caregiver. They can take out loans for the college thing, but it's a lot harder to get money for your retirement.

That being said, you'd be wise to save *something* for their post-secondary education. Children from low- to middle-income households are three times more likely to attend college and 4.5 times more likely to graduate if they know their parents are saving for it—even if you've only managed to save between $1 and $499. If you save any amount of $500 or more, their odds of graduating jump up to five times that of children whose parents have saved nothing.[67]

That marginal effort can really pay off. If you're from a low-income household, I'm going to encourage you to read this chapter as well as Chapter 4, which deals with nontraditional students, as you and your child will benefit from the information in both. If you're middle-income, this chapter is for you.

If you're from a high-income household, please save. It's one thing to not fund your children's education because you can't. It's another thing entirely to not pay for it because you don't want to do so. Your income will prevent them from qualifying for many scholarships and grants, so your own savings will be what gets them through school and rescues them from early financial struggles from which it could take years to recover.

ENCOURAGE EXTRACURRICULARS

Another way to invest in your child's future education is to get them involved in extracurriculars. Whether it be band, sports, Boy Scouts, or the forensics team, these are the things that are going to make them look well-rounded on college applications.

On top of getting them admitted, your investment in extracurriculars could end up scoring them some scholarship opportunities further down the road. Scholarships based on extracurriculars aren't necessarily income-based, which is good for children from middle-income families who may not qualify elsewhere. Of course, those from lower-income households can reap the benefits of extracurricular scholarships, too!

WAYS TO SAVE

When you're saving for college, you technically could just stash money into a savings account. But that's not necessarily where you're going to get the most bang for your buck—especially if you start saving when your child is young. Let's take a minute and review some of the savings vehicles that will help your money grow.

529 ACCOUNTS

There are two basic types of 529 accounts: prepaid tuition plans and college savings plans. Prepaid tuition plans essentially sell you tomorrow's credits at state schools at today's price. The idea is that you'll pay less money today, as tuition is likely to go up even more in the future. However, this locks your child into the state school system, and if they choose to cash out and use the money elsewhere, the interest you'll be rewarded with is nothing compared to what you could have earned with a college savings plan.

When you put money into a college savings plan, you're putting in post-tax dollars. That means that as your money grows, it will do so tax-free—as long as you end up using it for educational expenses. Known as college savings plans, these accounts allow you to withdraw the money you put in at any time. The interest you earn, however, will have to stay in the account until you're ready to use it for education. Technically, you could withdraw that interest, too, but you'd be hit with a 10 percent tax penalty.

Within a 529 college savings plan, you may have several investment options. These can run from extremely low risk—where you'll see the lowest amount of growth on your investment—to high risk, where you have a lot more potential for growth. Some plans also have age-based plans, which start out riskier, but as your child gets closer to high school graduation, get more conservative in order to protect your money, as you'll need it in the near future.

Every state has at least one 529 option, and each state's plan differs from the next. The great thing is you can buy across state lines. If you open an account in a state other than your own, you might miss out on some state tax benefits, but if the account has lower fees and better investment options than what is offered locally, it just might be worth taking the hit. Utah's 529 plan is extremely popular, so if you're shopping around, that may be a good place to start.

If you're concerned your children won't attend college, remember that the fact that you're saving at all increases the odds that they will. It may also help to know that you can transfer a 529 plan into another family member's name should your children turn out to be bound and determined that they can make it on their own without higher education.

All right. On to a more convenient scenario. You've done your job. You've put away money for your children's college education in a tax-advantaged 529 account, and they're ready to enter the halls of scholarship. Now there's just one question: What counts as an educational expense?

Luckily, the IRS lays it out in fairly plain language.[68] There were some changes in the tax code beginning in 2018, and this list reflects those changes:

- *Tuition at a post-secondary school which is set up to receive federal financial aid. (Remember that many two-year and vocational schools qualify under this definition. Some international schools even qualify.)*

- *Fees at those schools.*

- *Room and board. If you live off-campus, rent counts, too, but only up to the maximum amount that your college charges for room and board per month. If students on campus are paying $900/month and your rent is $1,000/month, you can only use $900/month from your 529 without incurring a penalty. You'll have to come up with the other $100 on your own.*

- *Books.*

- *Computers or other technology required for your courses. These must be explicitly required by the school—make sure you can find this requirement in writing.*

- *Internet access while enrolled in college.*

- *Up to $10,000 for tuition at a public, private, or religious elementary or secondary school.*

A note on the private school tuition thing: this part of the most recent tax bill was added at the last minute and passed by the skin of its teeth. Rewarding parents for sending their kids to private school is not a good thing, especially because those who have $10,000 in their 529 and feel okay using it for elementary or secondary school rather than holding onto it for college usually aren't hurting for money. Couple this with the fact that some states have tax codes which enable wealthy parents to receive tax credits for sending their kids to private school, and you've got a recipe for people profiting off of pulling their kids out of public schools.[69]

When children who can afford to go to private schools leave, they're leaving behind the children who can't. Generally, when a child leaves for private school, the funding that would have been used to educate them (and then some) follows the child. This leaves the children whose parents could not afford private school with less funding for their own education as the district sends off valuable resources with the wealthier child. This tends to happen most often with voucher programs rather than with the 529 change (as yet). Another major obstacle that keeps the children who need the education dollars the most deprived is the fact that transportation to private or charter schools is not always readily available—especially if the family cannot afford a vehicle of their own or cannot move their work schedule around to transport their child to and from school.

These 529 changes are likely a preemptive move to try to argue for the democratization of school choice—a method which has been repeatedly proven to fail those most vulnerable.[70] Keep an eye on this space in upcoming political debates and vote accordingly. It may not be the sexiest news story and may not even pop up in your Twitter feed, but it's crucial to the education of America's youth.

ABLE ACCOUNTS

If you have a disabled child, you may be extra unsure of whether they'll end up attending college. That doesn't mean you shouldn't save for their education, though. ABLE accounts are a relatively new type of financial account which allows you to save for your child's education and more.

Under the hood, they're 529 accounts, but according to the law, the list of qualified expenses is far vaster. Your child will be able to use the money for most day-to-day expenses, including things like rent even if they're not a college student. They will also be able to use it for things like home or vehicle modifications, employment training, health care expenses, and transportation, and the list goes on. If it improves or maintains their health and/or quality of life, it qualifies.

It is currently unclear if money saved in an ABLE account will hurt your child's chances of being awarded financial aid. Though these accounts do serve as a shelter for other asset tests such as Medicaid or SNAP benefits, there has not yet been any public word on how FAFSA calculations will handle these accounts. Keep an ear to the ground for any official policies announcements.

COVERDELL ESAs

The money you invest in a Coverdell Educational Savings Account will also not be taxed when you take it out for educational expenses. However, you can only save $2,000 per year in this account, and you will likely have to make some more complex investment choices on your own or with the help of a financial advisor. Your child will have to take the money out by age 30, though in some circumstances you can change the beneficiaries on these accounts, too.

TAXABLE ACCOUNTS

Technically, you can invest money outside of a 529 or Coverdell ESA, but you're going to get hit with taxes upon withdrawal whether your kid uses the money for college or not. One thing to make absolutely sure you do not do is to open a taxable investing account in your child's name. These are known as custodial accounts, and they will be weighted heavily when your child fills out the FAFSA—and not in your child's favor. Be sure to let well-meaning grandparents know not to do this as well. It can seriously hurt your child's chances of qualifying for federal financial aid, and many colleges use information from the FAFSA to make institutional financial aid decisions.

CANADIAN RESPs

Canada's Registered Educational Savings Plans (RESPs) allow you to invest for your child's education with post-tax dollars as your investment grows tax-free. Canada is super amazing and encourages parents to invest by offering a couple of grants which match a portion of your contributions. The Canada Education Savings Grant (CESG) gives you a 20 percent match on your contributions up to $500/year. The Additional Canada Education Savings Grant (ACESG) gives low- and middle- income families an additional 10 to 20 percent of the first $500 they invest every calendar year, too. In 2017, you could qualify for this additional grant with an income of up to $91,831.

These grants have a lifetime maximum of $7,200. That's a heck of a lot of free money for your child's education—at today's tuition rates, it would pay for more than a year of tuition at your average university. Keep in mind that these accounts can stay open for a maximum of 36 years and that if the money is not used in that time, the CESG and ACESG money may have to be returned to the government. Quebec, British Columbia, and Saskatchewan also offer similar grants at the provincial level.

Finally, if you are low-income, your child may also qualify for the Canada Learning Bond (CLB), which puts $500 in your RESP the first year your child is eligible and an additional $100 every year after that—as long as they remain eligible based on your income. The lifetime maximum on the CLB is $2,000.

APPLY FOR GRANTS

USA

Every year on October 1, the FAFSA opens. Your tax data will be pulled from the year before the year in which you are filling out the FAFSA. For example, if you apply on October 1, 2018, for the 2019-20 school year, calculations will be made using your 2017 tax return. The FAFSA opens up many potential grants for students—which are made up of money you don't ever have to pay back. Middle-income families should absolutely apply, even if you don't think your child will qualify for everything. Not only has there historically been money left over every year in Pell Grant funding, but filling out the FAFSA is often a prerequisite for being awarded any financial aid from your college.

In the past, the FAFSA was difficult to fill out. However, now that the government pulls your prior-prior year tax records and has so much data digitized, it's far less complicated. If you don't want your child seeing your tax data, fill it out yourself. Whatever you do, don't *not* fill it out, as that would severely stunt your child's ability to pay for school.

Flip back to Chapter 4 to learn about the grants offered via the FAFSA and how you may be able to find even more grants at the state level.

Canada

The Canadian government also issues grants for select demographics. Here are some to research for your child:

- *Grant for Full-Time Students*

- *Grant for Part-Time Students*

- *Grant for Students with Permanent Disabilities*

- *Post-Secondary Student Support Program (First Nations and Inuit students)*

- *Athlete Assistance Program*

More information on some of these programs can be found in Chapter 4.

APPLYING FOR SCHOLARSHIPS

Regardless of income level, your child should apply for scholarships. This piece of the college financing puzzle is especially important for those who come from middle-income families, though, as grants and need-based scholarships are going to be limited. Ideally, your child will go to college without incurring debt, and a good way to hedge against needing student loans is by applying for scholarships early and often.

To help us suss out the best ways to improve your child's odds of getting enough funding for post-secondary, I've tapped scholarship search strategist Ashley Hill. She says the number one thing your child should do in preparation for scholarship applications is to get leadership experience, as that's what nearly all scholarship committees are looking for.

"You don't have to have a career path specifically defined," says Hill. "Leadership experience is what's going to make you attractive to schools and scholarship judges. As they're looking at these applications and deciding who makes it to the next level, they want to see students who will be able to fit into the community there on campus, who are already active and showing those leadership qualities. They need to believe that you will develop more through your college years and that you'll continue making that impact."

She also advises that applicants not turn their essay into a brag list. If your child has accomplishments or awards they want to feature, they will have room to do so on the scholarship application; it's not appropriate in the essay. Instead, the essay should focus on those leadership experiences they've developed during their formative years.

EVERYTHING YOU'VE HEARD ABOUT THE IVY LEAGUE IS WRONG

When you think Ivy League, you probably envision people with loads of cash sending their snobby kids to some elite institution even though they may or may not deserve to be there academically. While that does sometimes happen, the truth is that Ivy League schools are most affordable for low- and middle-income families. This is because these institutions tend to have very large endowments which are used as institutional financial aid. One of the most generous programs is at Stanford, where you can expect to have all of your tuition and fees covered if your household income is $125,000 or less, though you can qualify for aid with a household income of up to $225,000.[71] For most American families, that means that if your child can get in, they can go for free.

Another myth you may have heard about Ivy League schools is that attendance doesn't really affect your salary over your lifetime; going to a state school is just fine. This isn't so much a myth as much as a whitewashed fact. Latinx and black students actually do see an overall increase in lifetime earnings after attending an Ivy League school, as do children of any race or ethnicity from low-income households or households where they are the first generation to graduate from college.[72]

To learn more about the affordability of and financial considerations around other types of colleges and universities, flip back to Chapter 4.

Hill encourages students to start applying for scholarships early. While she has seen hobby-based scholarships for younger children—in one case as young as age four—she notes that high school students are likely to encounter a lot of academic-based scholarships. These opportunities start younger than you may expect; Hill says your child should start applying as early as ninth grade. As you're encouraging your child to apply for these scholarships, she has some advice to prepare them—and you—for the process.

"Really encourage them to put in the work—to do what it takes," she says. "First, you both need to understand that they will not win every scholarship they apply for. This is extremely rare. If they get back a rejection letter, they should not be sitting there getting depressed. Encourage them to get back up, move forward, and apply for the next one. It's a numbers game."

To win at that numbers game, Hill strongly suggests setting up a system. She'd ideally like to see kids applying for five scholarships per week. If you think that's a lot, she recommends reframing the way you think about the process. Some kids go and get a job to save money for college. Rather than sending them outside the home, preparing yourself to look good on a scholarship application and then taking the time to fill out the applications could be a job in and of itself. If your child can get school fully funded in this way, their hard work will be worth the effort.

She also points out that most scholarship prompts ask the same or similar questions. To save time, your child will often be able to recycle essays, though they should always have a parent, teacher, or another set of eyes look over their essay before submitting it.

So you know how to prepare for scholarship essays and the importance of submitting a multitude of them, but where on earth are you supposed to find them?

Hill has a four-pronged strategy. If you're Canadian, substitute "provincial" for "state."

1. Stop in the guidance office of your high school, as they often have a list of local and national scholarships. You can also look at neighborhood organizations. These in particular are great because you tend to have much lower competition for them.

2. Look to organizations in your city. Whether that be the city government, local nonprofits, or affiliate chapters of national professional groups, you're likely to find college money where the competition is still relatively minimal at this level.

3. Check with similar organizations at the county level.

4. Try to find state-level scholarships. That could be via your state government, regional businesses, financial institutions, or nonprofits.

When you get to the national level, there tend to be more applicants and greater competition. That doesn't mean your child shouldn't apply, though—especially if the scholarship is issued by an organization that focuses on one of their hobbies, extracurriculars, or intended major.

TAKE ACTION 💲

- *Look at your investment vehicle options and decide which is best for your family. At the time of this book's printing, that's likely to be a 529 or ABLE account for most American families or RESPs for Canadian families.*

- *Do not open a taxable investment account in your child's name in America.*

- *Enroll your child in extracurriculars that match their interests and skills.*

- *Starting their freshman year of high school, encourage your child to apply for scholarships. Help them set up a system that will enable them to apply for at least five per week.*

- *Follow Hill's four-pronged strategy to find scholarships your child may qualify for. Better yet, have your child follow this four-pronged strategy independently.*

- *Talk to your child about the type of school they will go to and the type of costs they will incur. To prepare for this, flip back to Chapter 4.*

PART FOUR

WHEN ONE THING AFFECTS EVERYTHING

Warning: This section may contain triggers for those who have been through domestic or sexual violence or for those who suffer from certain mental health issues.

CHAPTER XVI
Cultural Norms Messed with My Brain

The financial struggles of dealing with mental health issues.

Mental health issues are not unique to women, but we are far more likely to deal with them than men. Women are diagnosed with major depression[73] and anxiety[74] disorders nearly twice as often as men. We're also more susceptible to bipolar II disorder[75] and are more likely to develop PTSD after a traumatic event.[76] Only 10 percent of those with eating disorders are male.[77] Then there are mental health issues that are completely unique to women, like postpartum depression.

Scientists aren't 100 percent sure why women suffer from mental health issues more than men, but they have a lot of theories. The first is hormones. The rate of depression among girls and boys is the same until we reach puberty, when we start getting depression at nearly twice the rate of pubescent boys. That pattern evens out around age 65, when men and women start having the same rates of depression again. This has led to the hypothesis that the hormonal changes we experience while going through our menstrual cycle increase the incidence of depression in women and that the increased risk is over when we've completed menopause.

Don't you love when someone blames your lived experience on your period? Yeah, me neither. It turns out that the menstruation theory isn't the only one out there. Equally as plausible are the effects of gender norms and social conditioning in our culture on women, as well as the higher incidence of not-so-great situations women face thanks to the kyriarchy.

We're going to break down some of these mental health conditions and the effects they have on our finances, because these effects are real and damaging. While they're not easy to overcome, we will also try to examine some tools that may help when used in conjunction with attention from a mental health professional.

DEPRESSION & ANXIETY

First, let's look at depression and anxiety. These two disorders are often two sides of the same coin. When your brain just can't handle anymore, it can either shut your whole life down by not allowing you to get out of bed—as with depression—or shut your whole life down by putting you on high alert about every last thing—like anxiety. The gender ratios of these two disorders are very similar.

If we look at the increased gender ratio onset as puberty, we could come to the conclusion that this was just hormones. However, doing so completely ignores what pubescent girls go through during this time period. In the preteen years, social structures start shifting, potentially changing or eliminating your social network just when it is becoming most important to you. You start developing breasts, which makes some girls feel shame and makes all girls victims of sexual objectification. When we flower, we start experiencing firsthand how the world places a heavier burden on our beauty within the context of our culture over the content of our character. We are socially conditioned to internalize our problems rather than manifesting our frustration through forms our male counterparts typically use as catharsis, such as rage.

We continue to deal with the whole beauty over brains thing our entire lives, working towards an ideal world while living in a reality that punishes us if we attempt to assert control, overpowers us through violence, and offers us less economic opportunity than our male counterparts.

We also need to be cognizant that gender is not binary; it's a spectrum. Sexual and gender minorities, including transgender, genderqueer, and nonbinary persons, experience depression and anxiety at twice the rate of the heterosexual population. When you come out or transition, you run a serious risk of damaging your existing interpersonal relationships and of subjecting yourself to bullying. Some deal with this by never coming out, while others do come out and then suffer massive social consequences. Not coming out has been tied to even higher rates of depression and anxiety, but that does not diminish the lived experience of those who have.[78] To me, all this indicates the strong influence society plays on our mental health.

I'm not a scientist. Maybe hormones are part of it. But reading about different theories and considering the fallacy of binary gender arguments has led me personally to believe that cultural influences are more powerful than periods.

These disorders can have a major effect on your finances. In one study which followed workers over the course of six months, those with depression dropped out of the workforce at a rate of 12 percent compared to a rate of 2 percent among their non-depressed peers.[79] It's also harder to keep track of your finances when you have these conditions, making it easier to overspend or miss payments on your bills or credit cards.

The very first thing you should do is seek mental health services. Reducing your symptoms will make everything in life—including your money—easier to deal with.

Until you get to that place, though, you can do things like setting reminders on your phone to pay bills, trying your best to find meaningful work as we discussed in Chapter 2, and/or creating a realistic budget that accounts for potential overspending.

PTSD

When we think of PTSD, we tend to think of soldiers. Most research dollars have been allocated to this population, and public empathy for them is high. This empathy is well-deserved.

But most soldiers who have sought and pursued treatment will tell you something most of us don't know: they're not the only ones who go through PTSD. In the next chapter, we'll talk about how 25 percent of the female population has experienced intimate partner violence (IPV). Experiences of physical, sexual, and psychological abuse are equally as traumatic as war, and all women—but especially those who have experienced sexual violence—are more likely to develop PTSD after trauma. Sexual and gender minorities are also at higher risk; they're 3.9 times more likely to develop PTSD than cisgender, heterosexual individuals.[80]

PTSD can have similar effects on your finances as depression and anxiety do, with a few fun extras. First, when you have PTSD, you're more likely to engage in hazardous behaviors like drug and alcohol abuse and risky sexual behavior. Purchasing substances can quickly lead to an overdrawn bank account, and all of these behaviors increase the odds that you'll incur serious and expensive medical problems.

If you have PTSD, you're also more prone to emotional outbursts, particularly angry ones, which can make things in the workplace incredibly awkward if you manage to hang onto your job. Another aspect of PTSD is hypervigilance, or the compulsive drive to head off any bad outcomes that may or may not be coming your way.

The effects of hypervigilance in particular have been studied, though only in the context of veterans to date. While soldiers aren't the population we're focusing on here, it's reasonable to assume we'll see a similar trend among survivors of domestic violence, IPV, and other traumas with PTSD once they are studied. A 2012 paper found that those living with PTSD are less likely to invest in stocks and mutual funds, presumably to hedge off the risk of losing money in the stock market.[81]

This is problematic for a few reasons. First, we know that women set their investment goals lower than men, so when we're talking about women with PTSD, we're likely to see this problem compounded, resulting in smaller retirement account balances. While riskier investments are in fact riskier, they also hold the most potential for returns. PTSD also tends to create greater employment gaps and more difficulty getting hired compared to the rest of the population,[82] so we're potentially talking about unnecessarily conservative investment strategies coupled with more years of not contributing to your retirement savings. This fact is even further compounded if you deal with employment discrimination due to your gender identity, gender presentation, or sexual orientation.

You're going to get sick of me saying this by the end of the chapter, but the number one thing you can do to help your economic situation is to seek mental health services. The work you do with a professional will serve you better than any money hack.

If you do have PTSD, though, sitting down with a financial professional may be more important than it is for other people. You have to find someone you trust, but once you do, you can explain to them that you are concerned that your investment strategy might be a bit conservative. If you're comfortable disclosing, you could even tell them why, though this is not mandatory. Often, the first meeting with a financial professional is free, and you don't have to be a billionaire to be able to afford one long-term.

POSTPARTUM DEPRESSION

Whether you've had a child or not, I want to tell you something: The post-birth experience isn't always a Hallmark-worthy experience. You may have your child, hold them in your arms, and think, 'This child isn't mine.' You might start hating yourself because of the lack of connection you feel with your child. You may spend time mourning the death of the person you were before you became a mother, now perpetually responsible for this tiny human being. With a lack of sleep on top of these potential mental health problems, you may start hallucinating or feeling suicidal.

This is the stuff of postpartum mood disorders such as postpartum depression, post-partum OCD, postpartum anxiety, and postpartum psychosis. It's not the experience we like to advertise to newly expectant mothers, but maybe it's one we should, because while 10 to 15 percent of women will go through this experience in their lifetimes,[83] those who do are often left with feelings of deep guilt that their newborn's early days didn't match the stories they heard growing up.

But it's not just the early days. Recent studies have shown that postpartum depression can first manifest anytime up until your child's fourth birthday.[84] If you're one of the women who has a delayed onset, you're less likely to receive a proper diagnosis and appropriate care.

To add insult to injury, those with a history of trauma, whether it be childhood abuse or intimate partner violence as an adult, are more likely to have depression or PTSD, and therefore more likely to experience postpartum mood disorders.[85] Sometimes one event in your life can unjustly affect everything else.

Postpartum depression can affect your personal economics in a lot of ways. It may be harder to return to work or hold down your job once you do. You may face problems similar to those mentioned earlier with ignoring bills or overspending in the name of self-soothing. And you should take a similar course of action: seek mental health services. Postpartum mood disorders can have dire consequences for you, your child, and your family—with effects well beyond the financial. But again, addressing your mental health will help you get to a place where you can even out your financial situation.

Know that there is no right way to experience motherhood or to be a good mother. The fact is that not every birth is joyous for everyone involved, and it's okay to feel whatever you need to feel. There are women who have been there before you, and in recent years, they've started to feel empowered enough to speak up and share their own stories. I'd encourage you to seek those stories out so you know just how many others share your situation. You are not alone.

I personally think we should have some type of conversation with all expectant mothers and their support network of friends and/or family just in case they do develop a postpartum mood disorder. If you and your support network are prepared for the worst, you'll have more hands at the ready to help you with baby, give you time to rest so your own body can recover, and give you the time you need to address any mental health issues that arise. Preparing doesn't mean it will definitely happen to you. It doesn't mean the birth of your child won't be that joyous Hallmark moment you've always dreamed about. But it does mean you'll have as much support as possible.

EATING DISORDERS

The beauty standards perpetually forced on us by the media, our peers, and even family members have real effects on our mental health. Of those with eating disorders, only 10 percent are men, demonstrating that while we need to address the root causes of their issues and get them the help they need, this is not a predominantly male issue.

Eating disorders can present in many ways. You may look in the mirror and see your body completely differently than the way it looks in reality. You may have anorexia and starve yourself. You may have bulimia and go through binges and purges. You may have another eating disorder that combines different components of all the other eating disorders. But however your disorder manifests, it's dangerous.

While beauty standards and social pressure definitely play a huge role in the development of these disorders, the underlying motivation is typically control. Maybe you can't control those kids bullying you at school, but you can control and manipulate your BMI. Maybe you can't control the abuse you're experiencing at home, but you can control how many calories you take in per day. You may not be able to control the fact that you just lost someone close to you, but you can control your decision of whether or when to stick your finger down your throat.

This type of control is not healthy, but it is logical. In fact, logic can take you pretty far down the yellow brick road when you have this particular type of mental health issue. You can even logic your way into thinking that your disorder is financially responsible. Let's take someone who is anorexic, for example. You might convince yourself that you're being fiscally responsible because you don't have to buy as much food. You spend less on lotion and other skin products because there's less surface area to cover when you're tiny (a.k.a. sick). It doesn't take as much of an inebriant to get you comfortably buzzed, and people are more likely to be generous towards you both socially and fiscally when you conform to the beauty standard that is held up by our society at large.

But make no mistake; eating disorders are expensive. All the money you save on food and lotion will pale in comparison to your hospital bills should you continue down this path. Eating disorders have been associated with sky-high rates of heart failure, suicide, early onset osteoporosis, pancreatitis, kidney failure, and amenorrhea (which is a fancy way of saying your menstrual cycle can get messed up—sometimes forever).

While you may choose not to eat or choose to overeat or choose to purge, you did not choose to have an eating disorder. Like everything else listed in this chapter, it is a mental health disorder and it is not your fault. But you need to believe it's a problem, because the sooner you get treatment, the higher your odds of survival. You can get one-on-one services with a therapist, and another great resource for those in certain regions of the United States is The Emily Program (emilyprogram.com).

You are beautiful. I'm sorry the kyriarchy made you feel differently and gave you all this suffering. But you can get healthy. Get the help you need, gorgeous, so you can grace this world with your presence for a longer period of time. We need you.

BIPOLAR II

While bipolar I affects men and women equally, bipolar II occurs far more frequently in women. The cause of bipolar disorders has not yet been identified, but we do know some of the financial effects. Abigail Perry, an author and customer service representative from the Phoenix area, shares her personal experiences with bipolar II.

"Luckily, bipolar II's manias are a lot smaller [than if you have bipolar I]," says Perry. "I wouldn't go completely crazy with spending, buying hundreds of dollars' worth of stuff. Usually, manias make me simply be a little stir-crazy and a little more inclined to spend money on things like a meal out or a piece of clothing. I think the worst manic spending I did was about $100— not a small amount, but nothing compared to some of the stuff you hear about."

Bipolar II does, however, have notably higher rates of depressive episodes with similar problems and solutions to those we discussed earlier in the chapter. To find out Perry's personal strategies for dealing with the financial issues that accompany depression, flip back to Chapter 6.

I'm sure there are other mental health issues that women encounter more often than men, but over the course of my work over the years, these are the ones I've run into most frequently. While more problems are thrown at us as women or gender minorities, that doesn't mean you are alone in your suffering. Seeking help is the first step to finding a community of people who can relate to your life experiences; and, of course, it is the first step to getting your money back on track.

TAKE ACTION $

- *Seek mental health care, first and foremost.*

- *If you struggle with depression and/or anxiety, set a flexible budget. Set alarms to remind you to pay bills on time, and try to either find meaningful work or ways to make your work meaningful.*

- *Do all the above things if you have PTSD, plus sit down with a trusted financial professional to make sure your investments aren't unnecessarily conservative.*

- *If you have an eating disorder, recognize that while your views on body size and frugality may be logical in isolation, they're illogical when you expand your view to look at the long-term costs of health care you're likely to need further down the road.*

- *If you are an expectant mother, ready your social network for any potential mental health issues that may arise after the birth. They may not come up, but this way you will have the help you need ready to go just in case, giving you a better chance of recovering sooner.*

CHAPTER XVII

Letters from the Home Front

***One in four women is affected by intimate partner
violence and economic abuse.***

Nour Naas grew up in an abusive home. She had never heard of
domestic violence. She didn't know there were resources to help.
As the years wore on, her mother tried to be proactive about it in
the only way she knew how: by belittling the problem. After years of
gaslighting—a practice in which the abuser convinces their victim
not to trust their own memory or judgement—it's understandable
that Naas's mother was best able to cope by pretending the problem
didn't exist. This isn't an uncommon reaction, and it's exactly why
abusers use the tactic.

On June 8, 2013, the years of abuse culminated in Naas's father
shooting her mother repeatedly in the chest. The shots continued
even after she had taken her final breath.

DOMESTIC ABUSE IS A PUBLIC HEALTH CRISIS

One in four women will experience intimate partner violence in their
lifetime. That's 25 percent of the female population experiencing
rape, unwanted sexual contact, physical abuse, and/or stalking.
The rate of occurrence in Muslim-American households like Naas's
is similar to the rate for the rest of the American population.
But Muslim women face added barriers in reporting. Because
Islamophobia is so pervasive in the West, there is added guilt
involved in reporting—a feeling of confirming the stereotypes and

giving fodder to those who would use it as an argument to further fuel hate towards the woman's own community.

"After my mother passed away, I didn't want to talk about it," says Naas. "The Muslim community is already targeted in so many ways through stereotyping and policies. I didn't want to add to it. There are really obvious ones like invading all these Muslim countries and occupying their lands, speaking about people from or in those countries as primitive, saying things like, 'We're there to save them,' and giving people this concept that these people are different from us, living in a backwards culture. But there are also stereotypes about Muslim men and women that make it hard to talk about. Men are supposedly violent and patriarchal; women submissive and in need of saving. You don't want to reinforce any of that."

Similar sentiments exist within the LGBTQIA+ community, where the rate of abuse is the same as it is in the heterosexual population. Because of long-standing prejudice, moral judgements, and oppression, the need to report and find resources can create a dilemma where you feel like you're choosing between your own personal safety and the reputation of your community.

Naas notes that Islamophobia is at times also in evidence at the institutional level, creating a mistrust of law enforcement that affects victims' decision to report. In the Muslim community, mosques have been surveilled by law enforcement. Racial profiling is widespread. The police haven't been on your side so far—why would they help now?

This same mistrust can be found in indigenous communities, where the rates of domestic violence and sexual assault are higher than for any other demographic. After centuries of colonialism, broken treaties, underfunded law enforcement programs on reservations, failure to enforce justice even when these crimes are reported, and the highest rates of interracial sexual violence in the country, it's again no wonder that professionals in the field are concerned that even these high numbers do not reflect an even darker reality, since it is suspected many women do not report.[86]

While we are focusing on women, it's important to remember that women can commit abuse, too, whether their partner is male or female. Again, the rate of occurrence is the same in the LGBTQIA+ population as it is in the rest of the population, and one in nine men have been victims of intimate partner violence regardless of sexual orientation.

We also need to be aware that your partner doesn't have to be hurting you sexually or physically to be abusing you. The gaslighting Naas's mother experienced is a form of psychological abuse. There is also verbal and emotional abuse to worry about. All of these nonphysical forms of abuse can do lasting damage to a person, as well. They may also precede sexual or physical abuse.

Domestic abuse and intimate partner violence are epidemic public health crises that are not being adequately addressed in any community, but when you add in any other types of oppression beyond your sex, reporting and getting the help you need without facing prejudice becomes decidedly more difficult.

RESOURCES

If you are in an abusive relationship, there is help out there. The following organizations are dedicated to connecting you with resources. Only phone numbers are provided here, though these organizations do have websites, too. Because cyber surveillance is another tactic commonly used by abusers, calling a hotline—especially on a phone to which your abuser does not have access—may be safer than looking for help online.

United States

National Domestic Violence Hotline (United States)
1-800-799-7233

National Sexual Assault Hotline (United States)
1-800-656-4673

Canada

Assaulted Women's Hotline (Ontario)
1-866-863-0511

Talk4Healing (Aboriginal women on and off reserve in Northern Ontario)
1-855-554-4325

Fem'aide (Francophone women in Ontario)
1-877-336-2433

Domestic Violence Helpline (British Columbia)
604-875-0885

Family Violence Infoline (Help in 107 languages in Alberta)
780-310-1818

Toll-Free Province-Wide Domestic Abuse Crisis Line (Manitoba)
1-877-977-0007

NWT Helpline (Northwest Territories)
1-800-661-0844

Nunavut Kamatsiaqtut Help Line (Nunavut)
1-800-265-3333

Domestic Violence Hotline (Québec)
1-800-363-9010

Hope Haven Transition House Crisis Line (Newfoundland)
1-888-332-0000

Nova Scotia Helpline
1-877-521-1188

Kaushee's Place (Yukon)
867-668-5733

Crisis Line (La Ronge, Saskatchewan)
306-425-4090

Domestic Violence Crisis Line (Moose Jaw, Saskatchewan)
306-693-6511

Domestic Violence Crisis Intervention (Prince Albert, Saskatchewan)
306-764-1011

Domestic Violence Crisis Line (Yorkton, Saskatchewan)
1-888-783-3111

Crisis & Suicide Line (Regina, Saskatchewan)
306-525-5333

If you need local resources, these hotlines should be able to point you in the right direction. If they can't, look up local shelters. If you're in the United States, you can also get in touch with the United Way, which commonly provides services which can be beneficial to survivors, by dialing 2-1-1.

ECONOMIC ABUSE

Economic abuse is part of the picture in 94 to 99 percent of domestic violence cases. That is to say that it's an almost inevitable experience for survivors.[87] If you've never heard of economic abuse, here are some of the ways it can present. Your partner:

- *Doesn't let you work.*
- *Sabotages your employment via stalking or another method.*
- *Doesn't let you get job training or education.*

- *Won't allow you to access the family finances.*

- *Gives you an "allowance" or makes you ask for money.*

- *Forces you to work for them or their business without paying you.*

- *Steals your identity.*

- *Threatens to ruin your credit history by withholding money needed to pay bills in your name.*

- *Racks up debt on joint accounts without discussing it with you.*

- *Drains the bank account without telling you.*

- *Forces you to take out a loan.*

- *Forces you to give them money.*

This list is not all-inclusive, and you can experience economic abuse whether you are the breadwinner or not. By controlling the finances, an abuser is controlling their victim's future and capability of leaving.

"Not having finances to leave your abuser is the number one reason women don't leave," says Naas. "They would have nothing to survive on. It's a source of a lot of people's depression when they're in that situation. When you don't have resources to leave, it just makes people feel hopeless."

There is no easy solution to this problem. You can stash cash at a trusted friend or family member's home, or you can try to find secretive ways to side hustle for a little money and reach out to local organizations for any resources that might be available, but you do need to keep in mind that every step you take does carry some risk. When an abuser starts to lose control, their behavior begins to get more extreme. In fact, the most dangerous time in an abusive relationship is when you're leaving. Even if your abuser has not been violent to this point, this is when those physical threats are most likely to happen and most likely to intensify to new levels.

For that reason, when you're preparing to leave, it's important to do so with the help of a trained professional. Having friends and family members by your side is encouraging, but 20 percent of all domestic violence related homicide victims are not the victims themselves, but rather friends or family members who have tried to step in.[88] Talk to someone trained in this field about your individual situation so you know how to do this as safely as possible.

LONG-TERM FINANCIAL EFFECTS OF ABUSE

Those who escape abusive relationships face great financial hurdles long after they've left. Your departure may have made you a single mother. Economic abuse may have stunted your education or career, making it difficult to jump back into the job market. Even if you are able to secure a job, your credit may have been destroyed, making it hard to get a loan or sometimes even housing.

On top of that, you're likely dealing with the very real aftermath of psychological, verbal, and/or emotional abuse, which can affect your ability to work and even where you spend your money.

"You're not in a state of mind to do anything because of those psychological scars," Naas explains. "There's a stigma attached to what a victim goes through. It can impact a person's work performance or their ability to bring in an income at all. Women who are in these situations will sometimes resort to drugs or drinking, etc., to cope with the pain. That ends up being where all their money goes."

The good news is that once you are safe and sound, there are steps you can take to make things a little better. They'll still be hard, but for the first time in a while, you're in a position where you can initiate some forward action.

First, seek mental health help if you don't already have it. A professional can help you work through the horror you've been through so that you're less likely to gravitate towards substances or risky behaviors and more likely to be able to handle day-to-day responsibilities that come with raising children and holding down a job.

If you don't have health insurance, know that some shelters will offer these services for free—even if you're not living there. Domestic abuse is also a valid reason for a special enrollment period on the health care marketplace. That means that even if it's not open enrollment season, you'll be able to apply for Medicaid or a marketplace plan for yourself and your children, thereby getting the insurance you need to see a professional outside of a shelter, should that option not be available or preferable.

The next thing you can do to get your finances on track is to look over your credit report. You can request a free copy from each of the three credit bureaus at annualcreditreport.com. If your credit was a part of the economic abuse, you're probably going to find a lot of negative line items on there.

If you're comfortable sharing your experience with your creditors, you can attempt to get these line items removed by writing goodwill letters. When you write a goodwill letter, you tell the creditor the number of your account, acknowledge that you did pay late, explain to them your extenuating circumstance (in this case, domestic abuse), and humbly ask them if they'd be willing to remove the reported line item given the circumstances, enabling you to move on with your life. If you have a restraining order, PFA, police report, or any other documentation, including it with your letter will go a long way towards legitimizing your request.

These letters don't always work. In fact, I'm the only person I know who has ever had their letter receptively received and gotten the negative line item removed. But if anyone has a case for hardship, it's you. It's worth giving it a try, as it could repair your credit report and open the door to borrowing or housing opportunities which can help you rebuild your life.

If your letters aren't successful, there is a light at the end of the tunnel—though that tunnel is admittedly long. Information on your credit report only stays there for seven years, except for bankruptcies, which can stay on there for ten. Some data, such as collection items, will start to affect your overall credit score less after a few years, though the information will still show up on your report.

That means that after 7-10 years, you could potentially have a clean slate. To keep it that way, do everything you can in the meantime to pay your bills on time and borrow only what you can afford to pay off. These are habits that could help you establish a healthy credit history and therefore a higher credit score at the end of that seven-year period.

If you need education or job training to make a meaningful salary in the employment market, flip back to Chapter 4 to find out how you can go to school for free. There are a lot of scholarship opportunities out there for abuse survivors, so be sure to include them in your search for free school money.

You can also apply for various assistance programs through the Department of Public Welfare. SNAP benefits (food stamps), health insurance, assistance paying your heating bill in the winter and sometimes your cooling bill in the summer, help with paying for childcare, Section 8 housing, and even cash benefits are just some of the programs that can help you get back on your feet. Some may even qualify for disability should they have severe anxiety, depression, PTSD, or another mental health disorder. Do not feel shame in using these programs. The reason they exist is to help people in situations like yours.

LOOKING FORWARD

Today, Naas is a political science major at UC Berkeley. About a year ago, she took her first training to be a domestic violence advocate and has been serving as a volunteer in her communities ever since. She has a special place in her heart for marginalized women—especially Muslim women. She is launching a new effort to create safe spaces for these survivors to share their stories and get help.

"Talking about domestic violence and making people aware can help get rid of the stigmas we have around it," she explains. "That way, if this is happening, you know you just need to tell someone that it's happening. We need a community of people who will help—who know it's not okay either. That attitude is not really there in the Muslim community or in most of the country, for that matter."

A major tactic abusers use is isolation. The more isolated a person feels, the less likely they are to reach out to their social network. For that reason, if you have a friend or family member who is going through this hellish experience, it's important to be there for them. It's important to not set ultimatums on your friendship such as, *"If you don't leave him by this date, I don't know what to do. I can't be there for you anymore."*

Leaving is hard, complicated, and dangerous. The best thing you can do to help is not to discipline, but to love and listen with full awareness that this process could take quite some time. Listen without judgement of your loved one's decisions while they're trying to find their way out of an impossible situation. And whatever you do, don't abandon them. You may be the last friend they have. Consider it an honor that they trust you enough to feel comfortable talking to you about it.

TAKE ACTION $

- *Review the list of signs of economic abuse. Learn to recognize them as you forge relationships.*

- *If you are in an abusive relationship or suspect that you may be, get professional help. You can do this by contacting one of the numbers listed in this chapter, seeking out 1:1 mental health services or contacting a local shelter.*

- *If you have recently left an abusive relationship, know that domestic violence is considered a valid cause for a special enrollment period under the Affordable Care Act. American women can get free insurance through Medicaid if they have little or no income regardless of the time of year they left their abuser.*

- *If you have already left, get a free copy of your credit report at annualcreditreport.com. (Everyone should be doing this anyway—regardless of the presence or lack of abuse in their lives.)*

- *If you find any negative line items on your credit report, attempt to have them removed by writing a letter of goodwill to your creditors.*

- *If you have already left and don't have the resources you need to provide for yourself, apply for welfare benefits. Zero shame. You're a brave, amazing human being who has survived more than most other people could. You will get back on your feet. You just need a temporary leg up while you get there.*

- *If you need an education or job training, flip back to Chapter 4 to see how you can get it for free.*

- *If you have a loved one in an abusive relationship, be there for them. Be there even though it is difficult to see someone you care about suffering, because leaving this type of situation is hard, dangerous, and complex. It might not happen as quickly as you wish it would. But you may also be the only person saving them from utter isolation.*

CHAPTER XVIII

My Life's Meaning Just Changed

The obstacles and triumphs of women raising special needs children.

Joyce Zahariadis's son was four years old when he was diagnosed with Autism. He wasn't just her second child—he was her second child on the spectrum. Her daughter—then seventeen—had been diagnosed with Asperger's Syndrome just five years prior. Shortly thereafter her two-year-old son was diagnosed with Autism, as well.

"For my second boy, I cried and felt like a failure as a parent," Zahariadis recollects. "I was in denial. I was mourning."

These feelings are extremely common when your child is diagnosed with a disability. Over time, you become more educated and learn to appreciate your child for who they are, and you understand that the disability is a huge part of what makes your child the beautiful human being they are. It's the reason Zahariadis prefers that people to refer to her children as Autistic individuals rather than individuals with autism.

"[Autism] is part of who they are," she explains. "Now I'm ready for my third son to be diagnosed and welcome it. Living with my boys has taught me more about Autism. With the right support, it changed us as parents—in a good way."

While Zahariadis has made major strides as parent, that doesn't erase the economic reality she and so many other mothers of disabled children face. When her first son was young, she faced the hard decision of becoming a homemaker or continuing in her career with her employer of 15 years.

"The number one reason I became a homemaker was because I knew deep down my first son was going to need my support," she says. "Even now, with therapy and school calls I can't work outside of the home. No way! No company will allow me so many call offs or days off."

WHY RAISING A CHILD WITH DISABILITIES IS A FEMINIST ISSUE

You may be reading this and thinking it's an odd thing to include. Aren't both parents affected when they have a disabled child? Why are we only focusing on the mamas?

Well, the fact of the matter is that this circumstance *doesn't* affect all genders equally—even when parents stick together. Zahariadis's story is not unique. As a Latina woman facing the gender pay gap and discrimination at work, her family decided it would be best for her to be the primary caretaker of their children. This is the same decision most families with disabled children make.

On average, mothers of children with health limitations make $7,566 less than mothers of children with no health limitations. And the reason we're featuring Zahariadis's story is that mothers of Autistic children make $7,189 less than mothers of children with other health limitations. These mothers are 6 percent more likely not to work outside of the home when compared to parents of non-disabled children, and when they do work, they average seven hours less per week.[89]

The same is not true for fathers of disabled children, whether those children are Autistic or not. The mother's predicament does affect the overall family finances, though: Families with Autistic children have an average household income 21 percent lower than that of families of children with other disabilities and 28 percent lower than households with children with no disabilities. The average income for these families is middle-income—high enough to prevent them from accessing Medicaid in some states, yet not high enough to compensate for the costs of perpetual therapies, potential housing and vehicle modifications, nutritional supplements, and all the other things Autistic children need to thrive.

These families are in a financial quagmire, and over the long term, mothers in particular face career stagnation and resume gaps from which it is difficult to recover. We could guess at the reasons mothers are more heavily impacted: they tend to raise children on their own more often, gender expectations default to the mother being the one to stay at home and play the role of caretaker, and the gender pay gap forces couples to be practical and make a hard fiscal decision that unfortunately further reinforces gender stereotypes, etc.

While all of those things are true, and none of them are the fault of the individual family but rather of the institutional structure we all live in, it's ironically not what I want to focus on in this chapter. By this point in the book, I'm sure that you get that there are complex issues so ingrained in our culture that they put those at the intersection of sexism, racism, ethnocentrism, and disablism at a disadvantage.

What I'd like to focus on instead are potential financial solutions for you if you're raising a special needs child. I'd also like to show everyone—whether you have a disabled child or not—that at the end of the day, money isn't everything. There are many ways to live a wealthy life.

FINANCIAL SOLUTIONS

When you have a disabled child, your number one financial solution is going to be getting your child onto Medicaid. You should attempt to do this even if your income is above the eligibility limit, since many states, including the Zahariadis' home state of Pennsylvania, allow disabled children onto Medicaid regardless of family income.

It's a harder-than-usual process that usually requires you to apply for and be denied SSI benefits in order to prove disability, but it's one that will allow your child to get the care they need.

Bear in mind that many private insurers will not cover many of the necessary benefits for Autistic children in particular. While some states now have protective laws mandating this coverage from health insurance companies, if you work for a large employer that self-insures its employees, your policy may not be covered by these state protections.

You should also be aware that not every state will let disabled children onto Medicaid if their family's income is above that eligibility level. Some notable examples—particularly for Autism—include Utah, Alabama, and Kansas. I have a guide I am happy to send to parents outlining each state's policies—just look for my contact information at the end of the book.

Even if your state does offer coverage, there may be a waiting list for waivers. Sometimes these waiting list are so long they make the program useless for some families. In Louisiana, disabled children whose applications were filed in 2004 to 2006 are just now being approved for Medicaid coverage under such waiver programs. In Maryland, advocates say that the waiting list is so long that you need to search out other coverage options as your child may age out of the system. Other states, like Pennsylvania, are good about getting these children coverage in a timely manner, even if working with the Department of Public Welfare is still a less-than-pleasant experience.

If your state offers coverage without making your child sit on a ridiculously long waiting list, you may face another potential conundrum: Are there enough qualified service providers in your area to get your child access to the care they need? If there aren't any occupational therapists in your rural town, for example, it doesn't matter how much Medicaid covers; your child isn't going to benefit.

In these situations, I offer a piece of advice that I know assumes a lot of privilege: Move. Move to a state that has more coverage. Within that state, move to a locale which has more than plenty of the service providers your child will need. Talk to other parents of special needs children before you decide on a school district, as not all school districts appropriately comply with the Individuals with Disabilities Education Act (IDEA), which entitles your child to a Free and Appropriate Public Education (FAPE), including accommodations.

I know this is a lot easier said than done. I know you may be leaving behind the support of family and friends when you leave your hometown. I know you may have to seek out new job opportunities and that saving the money to do so might take a while.

But in my opinion, it's something worth doing financially. Because if you stay where you are, either you're going to find yourself in a ton of medical debt very quickly, or your child is not going to be getting the services and medical attention they need to live a fulfilling life. I admire your tenacity if you choose to stay and fight the system, but if we're looking at raw finances, the long-term fiscal benefits of living in an accommodating area in a state which makes Medicaid coverage accessible tend to outweigh the struggle of making the move happen.

Life is about more than money, though. Know that I don't judge you regardless of your choice. Only you know what is best for your child and your family. I'm just here to talk about money.

While we're talking about money, let's talk about some areas where you may be spending it unnecessarily. Medicaid coverage is going to vary from state to state, but your child's policy may cover things you didn't think it would. You may be spending money out of your own pocket on these items when you could be stashing that money away for their future, your retirement, or even that much-needed family vacation. So go over your policy with a fine-tooth comb and see if your state doesn't offer the following coverages outside of the routine therapy session:

- *Diapers for disabled children over the age of 3.*

- *Dental services.*

- *Medical equipment (for both physical and behavioral health).*

- *Home and vehicle modifications.*

- *Nutritional supplements.*

- *Hypoallergenic formulas.*

- *Respite care, which provides you with a caretaker to give you a break from your own duties every once in a while, or to allow you to do something as simple as go grocery shopping.*

There are tons of other things Medicaid policies cover, too. Reading through your child's policy is going to be a task, but it's one that could save you a nice chunk of money by making you aware of the things insurance covers so you don't have to further strain your own household budget.

OTHER FINANCIAL RESOURCES

If you live in a state that will not allow your child to get on Medicaid, or if you need something that is not a covered benefit, there are some more funding options out there. The following organizations either offer grants nationally to parents of disabled children or give them the equipment or services they need directly free of cost.

First Hand Foundation
firsthandfoundation.org
(816) 201-1569

Challenged America
challengedamerica.com
(818) 907-6966

Kiddo's Clubhouse Foundation
kiddosclubhousefoundation.org
(678) 527-3224

Variety
usvariety.org
(323) 954-0820

There are even more organizations at the state and local level. Seek out these charities as they may be able to save you thousands and/or get your child equipment or care you couldn't otherwise afford.

MEANING VS MONEY

If you do a google search on raising a special needs child, you'll come across a lot of keywords and phrases like "coping," "struggles," "forever on duty," and "stress." These are all real things parents of special needs children encounter. After all, they are trying to do their best for their children within a system that has seemingly been built to exclude them. That's a tiring battle, and it can overwhelm your life.

However, that doesn't mean the source of these parents' exhaustion is their child. Rather, it's the exclusionary system we operate in which they are working so hard to change. This is done out of love. This is done through self-education. This is done through personal growth.

Perhaps this is sentiment is best encapsulated in Zahariadis's advice to other special needs parents.

"You are your child's advocate and cheerleader. You also have to be realistic and honest about your child's diagnosis. Get educated about state laws and your child's rights, and never give up. Don't only fight for your child, but for others. Create a community."

When you're battling a system, you're fighting for change not just for your individual child, but also for all the other children and families who find themselves in a similar situation. The community you find within that battle bonds you to others with shared experiences. These things are ingredients in the recipe for a meaningful life, which we have learned is far more important to our happiness than money.

"I love the patience and everyday joy raising them brings us," says Zahariadis. "I love how smart they are and how resilient they are. I love that my parenting is not boring at all. I have to do things differently, and I have come to the conclusion that this is an experience for my own growth."

Let's fight for economic equality for all. And until we reach it, let's be like Zahariadis and so many others, building meaningful lives full of personal growth throughout our struggle against the kyriarchy.

TAKE ACTION 💲

- *Attempt to get your child on Medicaid.*

- *If you cannot get your child on Medicaid, look at moving to an area where you can. This area should also have an adequate number of qualified service providers along with a school district known for properly accommodating children with special needs.*

- *If you cannot envision making the move, that's okay. You know what is best for your family better than I. While your finances may suffer as you struggle to get your child everything they need, your hard work and efforts may change the local political landscape for your own child and children to come.*

- *Reach out to grant-issuing organizations for things you're having trouble getting insurance to cover.*

- *Whether you have a disabled child or not, be like Zahariadis and work to effect the change you want to see in the world. Herein we can find meaning and build the contentment that so often seems to elude those who seek fiscal wealth only.*

ACKNOWLEDGMENTS

Although it is my name on the cover of this book, this work was very much a collaborative effort. I have so many people to thank—first and foremost, the women who were so open and giving of their time and stories. I learned so much from Nicole Lynn Perry, Jennifer Chan, Choncé Rhea, Hélène Massicotte, Ashley Hill, Nour Naas, Chatón Turner, Carol Graham, Terry Hekker, Taylor Milam, Aja McClanahan, Jackie Cummings Koski, Heather Watkins, Abigail Perry, Rebecca Neale, and Joyce Zahariadis. I am also extremely grateful to Amada Reaume for serving as a consultant regarding feminism within Canadian culture and Alice Wong for connecting me with enlightening and talented women within the disability community.

Sherrian Crumbley, Amber Christensen, and Molly Steadman served as fantastic sensitivity readers, bringing my own blind spots to light. Thank you for making sure I didn't put my mistakes into print and for educating me on ways to be a better ally.

There are many others who have reviewed my work and corrected my errors. Thank you to Brenda Knight for convincing me to write this book, guiding me as a first-time author through the process, providing me with constructive feedback on ways to improve my writing, and having extreme patience with me throughout the entire process.

Thank you to everyone at Mango, really. Elina Diaz created the cover art we all fell in love with, and Hannah Jorstad Paulsen and Ashley Blake exercised great patience and demonstrated expansive expertise as we worked through marketing of the tome. Countless others have helped with aspects of the book's writing, design, publishing, and marketing processes that I didn't even know existed and would have failed at had I attempted this same project via self-publishing.

This is not the first time I've been approached to write a book. But writing a book is a large endeavor, requiring a ton of time which may or may not be compensated fairly in the end. Over the years, Jana Lynch has served as a phenomenal advisor in the publishing industry, dissuading me from contracts that weren't a great fit and encouraging me to engage with publishers who treat their authors well. Because of her, I ended up working with Mango, and I am eternally appreciative for her guidance.

I'd be remiss not to acknowledge the sacrifices of my family as I worked to complete this manuscript. They accommodated a crazier-than-usual work schedule to allow me the time to put my thoughts and research on paper. They watched my children, tolerated my absence, and supported me in my moments of self-doubt. They are always there for me and are the reason I've ever had enough confidence to write at all.

Specifically, my children are to be thanked for this book. My interest in this subject area is partially due to my own lived experience and a desire to see true equality in the world, but these interests were magnified at the births of my children. This world is a difficult place, but it needs to be better for them. If my medium for making this world a better place—even in small ways—is writing, then they are the reason I put my fingers to the keyboard.

RESOURCES FROM THE WOMEN BEHIND THE STORIES

This book would be nothing without the numerous women who lent their time, perspectives, and stories of lived experience to its pages. I want to thank them from the bottom of my heart for making this tome possible.

Their perspectives are important and inspiring outside of the confines of these pages, though. I highly encourage all those reading to visit them and learn more on their individual websites or social media pages.

Carol Graham
www.brookings.edu/experts/carol-graham/
Happiness Around the World
ISBN-13: 978-0199606283

Choncé Maddox Rhea
mydebtepiphany.com

Nicole Lynn Perry
@transgirlinSEA on Twitter

Jackie Cummings Koski
moneyletters2.com
Money Letters 2 My Daughter
ISBN-12: 978-0989186001

Ashley Hill
collegeprepready.com

Heather Watkins
slowwalkersseemore.wordpress.com

Abigail Perry
ipickuppennies.net
Frugality for Depressives
ISBN-13: 978-1532842030

Chatón Turner
chatonsworld.com

Rebecca Neale
thepersonalfinance.lawyer

Hélène Massicotte
freetopursue.com

Joyce Zahariadis
mystayathomeadventures.com
On Joyce's site, you'll be able to find many free budget
printables—be sure to print them out!

Taylor Milam
taylormilam.com

Jennifer Chan
jennifertchan.net

Aja McClanahan
principlesofincrease.com
Aja has free books on her site that teach you how to get out of
debt, increase your income, and build wealth.

Terry Hekker
terrymartinhekker.com
Disregard First Book
ISBN-13: 978-1440131240

Nour Naas

nournaas.com
To get involved with Naas's new domestic violence project,
email dvpinquiries@gmail.com.

Brynne Conroy

My story is not the focal point of these pages, and I am not
vain enough to tell you my voice is as important as the rest of
these women. However, if you'd like to obtain a free copy of the
Medicaid guide mentioned in the last chapter, feel free to send
me an email at: femmefrugality@gmail.com. You can also visit
femmefrugality.com to keep up on my latest work.

BRYNNE CONROY

Brynne Conroy started writing about money when she didn't have any. As she found creative ways to save and earn, she told all of her friends about it. They were kind and patient with her but mostly weren't interested. Knowing there were other people out there who could benefit from what she was learning, she started sharing her knowledge on the internet, which led to birthing her award-nominated blog, Femme Frugality.

As the years wore on, her past work experience with oppressed populations started leaking out into her money musings. A determined person, she was building a better life for her family. But she started recognizing that we don't all face the same obstacles in our financial journeys. The bootstrap mentality may be what we all would like to believe in: that if we work hard enough, we, too, can achieve. The problem is that some people can work equally hard as others and still not get ahead. Because of this, Conroy believes it's important to explore the lived experiences of others so we can recognize and then address the problems they face, giving everyone equal access to opportunity.

Today, you can go back and relive the evolution of her writing on Femme Frugality and find more of her work in financial and parenting publications both in print and online.

ENDNOTES

1 Rimbey, Beth. "Achieving Balance in Work and Life," *Stanford Business,* https://www.gsb.stanford.edu/insights/achieving-balance-work-life. (August 22, 2017.)

2 Angelucci, Manuela, and Karina Córdova. "Productivity and Choice Under Stress: Are Men and Women Different?" *University of Michigan,* http://www-personal.umich.edu/~mangeluc/ChoiceUnderStress.pdf. (July 14, 2014.)

3 Holt-Lunstad, Julianne, Timothy B. Smith, and J. Bradley Layton. "Social Relationships and Mortality Risk: A Meta-Analytic Review," *PLOS Medicine,* http://journals.plos.org/plosmedicine/article?id=10.1371/journal.pmed.1000316. (July 27, 2010.)

4 Mendelsohn, Michael. "Positive Psychology: The Science of Happiness," *ABC News, https://abcnews.go.com/Health/story?id=4115033&page=1.* (January 11, 2008.)

5 Diener, Ed, Andrew T. Jebb, Shigehiro Oishi, and Louis Tay. "Happiness, income satiation and turning points around the world," *Nature Human Behavior,* https://www.nature.com/articles/s41562-017-0277-0.epdf. (January 2018.)

6 "Real Median Household Income," *Federal Reserve Bank of St. Louis,* https://fred.stlouisfed.org/series/MEHOINUSA672N. (September 13, 2017.)

7 Hamilton, Carol V. "Why did Jefferson change 'property' into 'the pursuit of happiness'?" *History News Network of The George Washington University,* https://historynewsnetwork.org/article/46460. (January 7, 2008.)

8 Tippett, Krista, host. "Successful Givers, Toxic Takers, and the Life We Spend at Work," *On Being,* https://onbeing.org/programs/adam-grant-successful-givers-toxic-takers-and-the-life-we-spend-at-work/. (October 22, 2015.)

9 Guven, Cahit, and Claudia Senik, and Holger Stichnoth. "You can't be happier than your wife. Happiness Gaps and Divorce," *Paris School of Economics,* https://halshs.archives-ouvertes.fr/halshs-00555427/document. (December 24, 2010.)

10 Schneider, Rachel, and Jennifer Tescher. "The Real Financial Lives of Americans." *Federal Reserve Bank of San Francisco,* http://www.strongfinancialfuture.org/essays/the-real-financial-lives-of-americans/. (2015.)

11 The Shriver Report, http://shriverreport.org/. (January 8, 2018.)

12 http://wyomingpublicmedia.org/post/more-native-american-women-taking-breadwinner-role#stream/0

13 "The Facts About Women and Poverty in Canada," Canadian Women's Foundation, https://www.canadianwomen.org/the-facts/womens-poverty/. (January 8, 2018.)

14 Oliver, Melvin L. and Thomas M. Shapiro. *Black Wealth/White Wealth.* 1995. Routledge, 2006.

15 "Usual Weekly Earnings of Wage and Salary Workers Fourth Quarter 2017," Bureau of Labor Statistics, https://www.bls.gov/news.release/pdf/wkyeng.pdf. (January 17, 2018.)

16 "Does education pay? A comparison of earnings by level of education in Canada and its provinces and territories," Statistics Canada, http://www12.statcan.gc.ca/census-recensement/2016/as-sa/98-200-x/2016024/98-200-x2016024-eng.cfm. (November 29, 2017.)

17 Michael Mitchell, Michael Leachman and Kathleen Masterson, "Funding Down, Tuition Up," Center on Budget and Policy Priorities, https://www.cbpp.org/research/state-budget-and-tax/funding-down-tuition-up. (August 15, 2016.)

18 "Average Published Undergraduate Charges by Sector and by Carnegie Classification, 2017-18," College Board, https://trends.collegeboard.org/college-pricing/figures-tables/average-published-undergraduate-charges-sector-2017-18. (February 2, 2018.)

19 "Tuition fees for degree programs, 2017/2018," Statistics Canada, http://www.statcan.gc.ca/daily-quotidien/170906/dq170906b-eng.htm. (September 6, 2017.)

20 "Canada Grant for Full-Time Students," Government of Canada, https://www.canada.ca/en/employment-social-development/services/education/grants/full-time.html. (February 7, 2018.)

21 "Canada Grant for Full-Time Students with Dependants," Government of Canada, https://www.canada.ca/en/employment-social-development/services/education/grants/dependants.html. (July 28, 2016.)

22 "The Majority of Children Live with Two Parents, Census Bureau Reports," *United States Census Bureau,* https://www.census.gov/newsroom/press-releases/2016/cb16-192.html. (November 17, 2016.)

23 Scotti, Monique. "The Canadian Household is Changing: More single dads, more same-sex parents, fewer young families," *Global News*, https://globalnews.ca/news/3641761/census-canada-single-dads-same-sex-parents-young-families/. (August 2, 2017.)

24 Brody, Lauren Smith. *The Fifth Trimester: The Working Mom's Guide to Style, Sanity, and Big Success After Baby*. New York City: Knopf Doubleday Publishing Group, 2017. Print.

25 "EI Maternity and Parental Benefits - Overview," *Government of Canada,* https://www.canada.ca/en/services/benefits/ei/ei-maternity-parental.html. (March 23, 2018.)

26 "Wage Earner," *Québec Parental Insurance Plan*, http://www.rqap.gouv.qc.ca/travailleur_salarie/choix_en.asp. (March 23, 2018.)

27 "Dis." Origin and Etymology of DIS-. *Merriam-Webster Dictionary*, https://www.merriam-webster.com/dictionary/dis. (June 12, 2018.)

28 Schilt, Kristen and Matthew Wiswall. "Before and After: Gender Transitions, Human Capital, and Workplace Experiences," *The B.E. Journal of Economic Analysis and Policy*, https://www.ilga-europe.org/sites/default/files/before_and_after_-_gender_transitions_human_capital_and_workplace.pdf. (2008.)

29 "Racial Wage Gap," *The Conference Board of Canada*, http://www.conferenceboard.ca/(X(1)S(b35pb4ocsojkzk3g14ym3o2z))/hcp/provincial/society/racial-gap.aspx. (March 13, 2018.)

30 Lambert, Brittany and Kate McInturff. "Making Women Count: The Unequal Economics of Women's Work," *Oxfam Canada*, https://www.policyalternatives.ca/sites/default/files/uploads/publications/National%20Office/2016/03/Making_Women_Count2016.pdf. (March 2016.)

31 Rocheleau, Matt. "Chart: The percentage of women and men in each profession," *Boston Globe*, https://www.bostonglobe.com/metro/2017/03/06/chart-the-percentage-women-and-men-each-profession/GBX22YsWl0XaeHghwXfE4H/story.html. (March 7, 2017.)

32 "Occupational Employment and Wages, May 2017, 11-3071 Transportation, Storage, and Distribution Managers," *Bureau of Labor Statistics*, https://www.bls.gov/oes/current/oes113071.htm. (March 30, 2018.)

33 Shierholz, Heidi. "Low Wages and Scant Benefits Leave Many In-Home Workers Unable to Make Ends Meet," *Economic Policy Institute*, https://www.epi.org/publication/in-home-workers/. (November 26, 2013.)

34 "Quarterly Census of Employment and Wages," *Bureau of Labor Statistics*, https://data.bls.gov/cew/apps/table_maker/v4/table_maker.htm#type=1&year=2017&qtr=4&own=5&ind=814&supp=0. (June 2, 2016.)

35 Maddalone, Guy. *How to Hire a Nanny: Your Complete Guide to Finding, Hiring, and Retaining Household Help, 3rd ed.* Pennsauken, New Jersey: BookBaby. (March 23, 2017.)

36 Artz, Benjamin, Amanda H. Goodall and Andrew J. Oswald. "Do Women Ask?" *Warwick Economics*, https://warwick.ac.uk/fac/soc/economics/research/workingpapers/2016/twerp_1127_oswald.pdf. (September 2016.)

37 Brody, Lauren Smith. *The Fifth Trimester: The Working Mom's Guide to Style, Sanity, and Big Success After Baby*. New York City: Knopf Doubleday Publishing Group, 2017. Print.

38 "Global Gender Gap Report 2017," *World Economic Forum*, http://reports.weforum.org/global-gender-gap-report-2017/results-and-analysis/. (November 2, 2017.)

39 Anderssen, Erin. "Seven things to know about Canada's new parental leave benefits," *The Globe and Mail,* https://www.theglobeandmail.com/life/parenting/mothers-day/federal-budget-2017-maternity-leave/article34414374/. (May 4, 2017.)

40 Artz, Benjamin, Amanda H. Goodall, and Andrew J. Oswald. "Do Women Ask?" *Warwick Economics,* https://warwick.ac.uk/fac/soc/economics/research/workingpapers/2016/twerp_1127_oswald.pdf. (July 2016.)

41 "The 2016 State of Women-Owned Businesses Report," *American Express OPEN,* http://www.womenable.com/content/userfiles/2016_State_of_Women-Owned_Businesses_Executive_Report.pdf. (April 2016.)

42 Haimerl, Amy. "The fastest-growing group of entrepreneurs in America," *Fortune,* http://fortune.com/2015/06/29/black-women-entrepreneurs/. (June 29, 2015.)

43 Gaille, Brandon. "39 Shocking LGBT Discrimination Statistics," *Bradon Gaille,* https://brandongaille.com/37-shocking-lgbt-discrimination-statistics/. (May 20, 2017.)

44 Dutch, H. Waverly, Ph.D., Vivienne Ming, Ph.D., Mary E. Shea, Ph.D., and Chris Sinton. "The State of LGBT Entrepreneurship in the U.S.," *StartOut,*

https://startout.org/wp-content/uploads/2018/03/State_of_LGBT_Entrepreneurship.pdf. (July 2016.)

45 "Frequently Asked Questions," *Small Business Association Office of Advocacy,* https://www.sba.gov/sites/default/files/FAQ_Sept_2012.pdf. (September 2012.)

46 "Women in Law in Canada and the U.S.," *Catalyst,*

http://www.catalyst.org/knowledge/women-law-canada-and-us. (April 19, 2017.)

47 "The High Price of Silence: Analyzing the Business Implications of an Under-Vacationed Workforce," *Project Time Off,* https://projecttimeoff.com/reports/the-high-price-of-silence-analyzing-the-business-implications-of-an-under-vacationed-workforce/. (October 12, 2016.)

48 Robinson, Joe. "The Secret to Increased Productivity: Taking Time Off," *Entrepreneur,* https://www.entrepreneur.com/article/237446. (October 2014.)

49 "Transgender Military Service in the United States," The Williams Institute, http://williamsinstitute.law.ucla.edu/wp-content/uploads/Transgender-Military-Service-May-2014.pdf. (May 2014).

50 Jamie M. Grant, Lisa A Mottet, and Justin Tanis, "Injustice at Every Turn: A Report of the National Transgender Discrimination Survey," National Center for Transgender Equality, https://transequality.org/sites/default/files/docs/resources/NTDS_Exec_Summary.pdf. (March, 26, 2018.)

51 "May 2017 Metropolitan and Nonmetropolitan Area Occupational Employment and Wage Estimates: Seattle-Tacoma-Bellevue, WA," Bureau of Labor Statistics, https://www.bls.gov/oes/current/oes_42660.htm#00-0000. (March 26, 2018.)

52 "May 2017 Metropolitan and Nonmetropolitan Area Occupational Employment and Wage Estimates: San Diego-Carlsbad, CA," Bureau of Labor Statistics, https://www.bls.gov/oes/current/oes_41740.htm#00-0000. (March 26, 2018.)

53 "May 2017 Metropolitan and Nonmetropolitan Area Occupational Employment and Wage Estimates: New York-Newark-Jersey City, NY-NJ-PA," Bureau of Labor Statistics, https://www.bls.gov/oes/current/oes_35620.htm#00-0000. (March 26, 2018.)

54 Aboujaoude, Elias, Ronald J. Faber, Lorrin M. Koran, Michael D. Large, and Richard T. Serpe. "Estimated Prevalence of Compulsive Buying Behavior in the United States," *Psychiatry Online,* https://ajp.psychiatryonline.org/doi/10.1176/ajp.2006.163.10.1806. (October 1, 2006.)

55 "First Marriages in the United States: Data From the 2006–2010 National Survey of Family Growth," National Center for Health Statistics, https://www.cdc.gov/nchs/data/nhsr/nhsr049.pdf. (March 22, 2012.)

56 "4 in 10 first marriages end in divorce: report," CBC News, http://www.cbc.ca/news/canada/4-in-10-1st-marriages-end-in-divorce-report-1.953894. (October 4, 2010.)

57 "Facts + Statistics: Homeowners and renters insurance," Insurance Information Institute, https://www.iii.org/fact-statistic/facts-statistics-homeowners-and-renters-insurance. (February 28, 2018.)

58 "A Few Facts at the Household Level," National Fire Protection Association, https://www.nfpa.org/News-and-Research/Fire-statistics-and-reports/Fire-statistics/Fires-by-property-type/Residential/A-few-facts-at-the-household-level. (July 2009.)

59 "World Population Prospects," United Nations, https://esa.un.org/unpd/wpp/DataQuery/, (January 12, 2018).

60 "Canadian Survey on Disability, 2012," Statistics Canada, http://www.statcan.gc.ca/daily-quotidien/160705/dq160705b-eng.htm. (July 5, 2016.)

61 "The Faces and Facts of Disability," Social Security Administration, https://www.ssa.gov/disabilityfacts/facts.html. (February 28, 2018.)

62 Cornfield, Jill. "Survey: Just 4 in 10 Americans have savings they'd rely on in an emergency," *Bankrate,* https://www.bankrate.com/finance/consumer-index/money-pulse-0117.aspx. (July 12, 2017.)

63 Braga, Breno, Emma Kalish, Singe-Mary McKernan, and Caroline Ratcliffe. "Thriving Residents, Thriving Cities," *Urban Institute,* https://www.urban.org/sites/default/files/publication/79776/2000747-thriving-residents-thriving-cities-family-financial-security-matters-for-cities.pdf. (April 2016.)

64 Romo, Lynsey K., and Anita L. Vangelisti. "Money Matters: Children's Perceptions of Parent-Child Financial Disclosure," *Eastern Communication Association,* https://www.tandfonline.com/doi/figure/10.1080/08824096.2014.907147?scroll=top&needAccess=true. (April 25, 2014.)

65 "Who's the Better Investor: Men or Women?" *Fidelity,* https://www.fidelity.com/about-fidelity/individual-investing/better-investor-men-or-women. (May 18, 2017.)

66 "Retirement Fitness Survey." Wells Fargo. 2010.

67 Elliott, William, Ilsung Nam, and Hyun-a Song. "Relationships Between College Savings and Enrollment, Graduation and Student Loan Debt," *Washington University in St. Louis,* https://csd.wustl.edu/publications/documents/rb13-09.pdf. (March 2013.)

68 "529 Plans: Questions and Answers," *The Internal Revenue Service,* https://www.irs.gov/newsroom/529-plans-questions-and-answers. (February 20, 2018.)

69 Strauss, Valerie. "Three big problems with school 'choice' that supporters don't like to talk about," *The Washington Post,* https://www.washingtonpost.com/news/answer-sheet/wp/2017/05/03/three-big-problems-with-school-choice-that-supporters-dont-like-to-talk-about/?utm_term=.fcc1aaa5f1b0. (May 3, 2017.)

70 Rotherham, Andrew J. "A Lousy School Choice: Why the new tax break for private schools is such bad policy," *US News & World Report,* https://www.usnews.com/opinion/knowledge-bank/articles/2017-12-27/the-new-529-private-school-tax-break-is-bad-policy. (December 27, 2017.)

71 "The Parent Contribution," *Stanford University,* https://financialaid.stanford.edu/undergrad/how/parent.html. (June 7, 2017.)

72 Dale, Stacy Berg, and Alan B. Krueger. "Estimating the Payoff to Attending a More Selective College: An Application of Selection on Observables and Unobservables," *The National Bureau of Economic Research,* http://www.nber.org/papers/w7322. (August 1999.)

73 "Depression in women: Understanding the gender gap," *The Mayo Clinic,* https://www.mayoclinic.org/diseases-conditions/depression/in-depth/depression/art-20047725. (January 16, 2016.)

74 Brayne, Carol, Rianne van der Linde, Louise Lafortune, and Olivia Remes. "A systemic review of reviews on the prevalence of anxiety disorders in adult populations," *University of Cambridge,* https://onlinelibrary.wiley.com/doi/abs/10.1002/brb3.497. (June 5, 2016.)

75 Arnold, LM. "Gender differences in bipolar disorder," *The Psychiatric Clinics of North America,* https://www.ncbi.nlm.nih.gov/pubmed/14563100. (September 26, 2003.)

76 "Women, Trauma and PTSD," *US Department of Veteran Affairs,* https://www.ptsd.va.gov/public/PTSD-overview/women/women-trauma-and-ptsd.asp. (August 13, 2015.)

77 "Eating Disorder Facts," *The Emily Program,* https://www.emilyprogram.com/about-eating-disorders/eating-disorder-facts. (May 14, 2018.)

78 Hayes-Skelton, Sarah A., Ph.D., and David W. Pantalone, Ph.D. "Anxiety and Depression in Sexual and Gender Minority Individuals," *Anxiety and Depression Association of America,* https://adaa.org/sexual-gender-minority-individuals. (May 15, 2018.)

79 Adler, David A., M.D., Ernst R. Berndt, Ph.D., Hong Chang, Ph.D., Maggie Y. Hood, M.P.H., Leueen Lapitsky, M.P.H., Debra Lerner, Ph.D., M.S., Thomas J. McLaughlin, Ph.D., Carla Perissinotto, M.A., John Reed, M.D., and William H. Rogers, Ph.D. "Unemployment, Job Retention, and Productivity Loss Among Employees With Depression," *American Psychiatric Association,* https://ps.psychiatryonline.org/doi/abs/10.1176/appi.ps.55.12.1371. (December 1, 2004.)

80 Austen, S. Bryn, Sc.D., Heather L. Corliss, Ph.D., Karestan C. Koenen, Ph.D., Andrea L. Roberts, Ph.D., and Margaret Rosario, Ph.D. "Elevated Risk of Posttraumatic Stress in Sexual Minority Youths: Mediation by Childhood Abuse and Gender Nonconformity," *American Journal of Public Health,* https://ajph.aphapublications.org/doi/abs/10.2105/AJPH.2011.300530. (July 11, 2012.)

81 Bogan, Vicki I., David R. Just, and Brian Wansink. "Do Psychological Shocks Affect Financial Risk Taking Behavior? A Study of U.S. Veterans," *Western Economic Association International,* http://bogan.dyson.cornell.edu/doc/research/COEP2013.pdf. (July 3, 2013.)

82 "PTSD, Work, and Your Community," *US Department of Veteran Affairs,* https://www.ptsd.va.gov/public/community/ptsd-work-and-community.asp. (August 13, 2015.)

83 Stone, Katherine. "How Many Women Get Postpartum Depression? The Statistics on PPD," *Postpartum Progress,* http://www.postpartumprogress.com/how-many-women-get-postpartum-depression-the-statistics-on-ppd. (May 14, 2018.)

84 Brown, SJ, D Gartland, F Mensah, and H Woolhouse. "Maternal depression from early pregnancy to 4 years postpartum in a postpartum pregnancy cohort study: implications for primary care health," *British Journal of Gynecology,* https://obgyn.onlinelibrary.wiley.com/doi/abs/10.1111/1471-0528.12837. (May 21, 2014.)

85 Liberzon, Israel, Lisa Kane Low, Maria Muzik, David L. Ronis, Julia S. Seng, and Mickey Sperlich. "Childhood abuse history, posttraumatic stress disorder, postpartum mental health and bonding: A prospective cohort study," *J Midwifery Women's Health,* https://www.ncbi.nlm.nih.gov/pmc/articles/PMC3564506/. (January 1, 2014.)

86 "The Facts on Violence Against American Indian/Alaskan Native Women," *Futures Without Violence,* https://www.futureswithoutviolence.org/userfiles/file/Violence%20Against%20AI%20AN%20Women%20Fact%20Sheet.pdf. (May 14, 2018.)

87 "Quick Guide: Economic and Financial Abuse," *National Coalition Against Domestic Violence,* https://ncadv.org/blog/posts/quick-guide-economic-and-financial-abuse. (April 12, 2017.)

88 "Statistics," *National Coalition Against Domestic Violence,* https://ncadv.org/learn-more/statistics. (May 14, 2018.)

89 Cidav, Zuleyha, David S. Mandell, and Steven C. Marcus. "Implications of Childhood Autism for Parental Employment and Earnings," *Pediatrics,* https://www.ncbi.nlm.nih.gov/pmc/articles/PMC3356150/. (April 2012.)